Young W
2004 POETRY CO

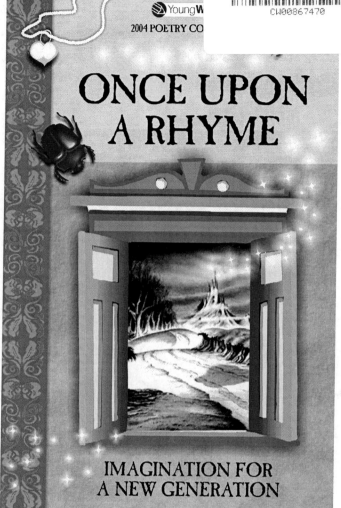

ONCE UPON A RHYME

IMAGINATION FOR
A NEW GENERATION

Lancashire Vol III

Edited by Chris Hallam

James
Tuohy

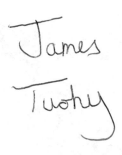

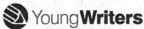 Young**Writers**

First published in Great Britain in 2004 by:
Young Writers
Remus House
Coltsfoot Drive
Peterborough
PE2 9JX
Telephone: 01733 890066
Website: www.youngwriters.co.uk

SB ISBN 1 84460 557 4

Foreword

Young Writers was established in 1991 and has been passionately devoted to the promotion of reading and writing in children and young adults ever since. The quest continues today. Young Writers remains as committed to engendering the fostering of burgeoning poetic and literary talent as ever.

This year's Young Writers competition has proven as vibrant and dynamic as ever and we are delighted to present a showcase of the best poetry from across the UK. Each poem has been carefully selected from a wealth of *Once Upon A Rhyme* entries before ultimately being published in this, our twelfth primary school poetry series.

Once again, we have been supremely impressed by the overall high quality of the entries we have received. The imagination, energy and creativity which has gone into each young writer's entry made choosing the best poems a challenging and often difficult but ultimately hugely rewarding task - the general high standard of the work submitted amply vindicating this opportunity to bring their poetry to a larger appreciative audience.

We sincerely hope you are pleased with our final selection and that you will enjoy *Once Upon A Rhyme Lancashire Vol III* for many years to come.

Contents

Bedford Hall Methodist Primary School

Catforth Primary School

Laura Oldfield (6)	22
Gabriella Giannoccaro (10)	23
Kieran Hamilton (9)	23
Ashleigh Butler (10)	24
Ian Terrell (11)	24
Kathy Stones (9)	25
Emily Terrell (8)	25
Jacob Odix (10)	26
Harriet Parkinson (10)	26
Nicola Birch (8)	27
Connor Hardie (9)	27
Alexandra Butcher (9)	28
Harry Rose (9)	28
Beth Odix (7)	29

Caton Community Primary School

Rachael Murby (9)	29
Kathryn Mills (10)	30
Ella Jarman (9)	31
Stacy Brown (9)	31
Emma Hodgson (10)	32
Katie Harding (10)	32
Oliver Parsons (10)	33
Ryan Leonard (9)	33
Sarah Murby (10)	34
Amy France (9)	34
David Riley (10)	35
Samantha Haggan (9)	36

Christ Church CE Primary School

Alicia Clegg (7)	37
Elliot Howley (9)	38
Robyn Warrington (8)	38
Heather Johnson (11)	39
Matthew Byrom (7)	39
Emily Duthie (9)	40
Aimee Mahoney (8)	40
Holly Espie (11)	41
Jodie Anchor (9)	41
Sam Reynolds (11)	42

Robert McLintock (11)	42
Rebecca Connell (11)	43
Frances Taylor (9)	43
Rachel Coope (10)	44
Lauren Warrington (10)	44
Sophie Johnson (11)	45

Dolphinholme CE Primary School

Andrew Lee (10)	45
Natasha Ball (10)	46
Rebecca Hodgson (10)	47
Jillian Hayhurst (10)	47
Jonathan Baines (10)	48
Liam Withers (11)	48
Class 5	49
James Bland (11)	49
Oliver Winder (11)	50
Kirsty Mudd (11)	50
Jacky King (10)	51
Jessica Wilson (10)	51

Hamer CP School

Mohammed Oussama (10)	52
Lewis Clark (10)	52
Tariq Mohammed (11)	53
Rose Tomlin (11)	53
Farah Imtiaz (11)	54
Sophie Handley (11)	54
Saqib Ishaq (9)	55
Adam Dunnington (11)	55
Nafisah Saleem (10)	56
Saleha Begum (10)	56
Chantelle Deloughrey (11)	57
Aysha Ahmad (11)	58

High Bentham CP School

Rowan Turnbull-Brown (9)	58
Elsa Priestley (10)	59
Shannon O'Hagan (10)	59
Beccy Lloyd (10)	59
Jack Harrison (10)	60

Ben Millings (9)	60
David Adam (10)	60
Lauren O'Hagan (9)	61
Andrew Procter (10)	61
James Tuohy (10)	61
Hattie Clay (9)	62
Lewis Sharpe (10)	62
Isaac Dennis (9)	62
Stephanie Cowgill (10)	63
David Lester (10)	63
Faye Cook (10)	63
Jordan Armstrong (9)	64
Sara Carter (10)	64
Connor Hall (9)	64
Hayley Mace (9)	65
Liam Ellershaw (10)	65

Mayfield Primary School

Alison Clark (10)	65
Charlotte Salt (11)	66
Rebecca Hulley (11)	66
Sophie Lees (11)	67
Samantha Irving (10)	67
Patrick Tobin (11)	68
Nicolle Burlison (11)	68
Kelsey Swales (10)	69
Rachel Eaton (11)	69
Rosie Sutton (10)	70
Mark Holme (10)	70
Katie Cartwright (11)	71
Matthew Goddard (11)	71
Jack Herring (10)	72
Connor Grady (10)	72
Laura Williams (11)	73
Rachel Gartside (10)	73
Callum Entwistle (10)	73
Rebecca Bellingham (10)	74
Sarah Davies (10)	74
Leoni Grenfell (10)	75
Hayley Coombes (10)	75
Lexi Ogden (10)	76

Katie Rourke (10)   76
Heather Brooks (10)   77
Shelby Newton (9)   77
Liam McCallion (10)   78

Our Lady & St Anselm's RC Primary School
Jack Broxup (10)   78
Nathan Fowles (11)   79
Bethany O'Malley (10)   79
Hannah Robinson (10)   80
Lois Vail (10)   80
Kieran Ryan (11)   81
Alex Foster (10)   81
Jessica Claxton (10)   82
Megan Hall (10)   82
Michaela McDonald (10)   83
Liam Blackmore (10)   83
Rory Troughton (10)   84
Amber Whitehead (10)   84
Harry Peters (10)   85
Jessica Wilkinson (10)   85

Ribby With Wrea Endowed CE Primary School
Michael Yaxley (9)   86
Sophie Jones (10)   87
Danielle Keady (9)   88
Thomas Leach (10)   88
Alexandra Hodson (11)   89
Laura Fenton (10)   89
Jack Warrington (11)   90
Thomas Yaxley (11)   90
Daniel Hinde (11)   91
Peter Pilkington (11)   91
Joe Walsh (10)   92
Hailey Voyle (11)   93
Kieran McSpirit (11)   94
Patrick Parr (10)   95
Ben Jones-Dale (10)   96
Helen Cropper (10)   97
Ashley Harding (11)   98
Rachel Cara (10)   99

St James' CE Primary School, Chorley

William Hargreaves (11)	99
Sam Tait (10)	100
John Worthington (9)	100
Philip Robert Smalley-Morris (11)	101
Andrew McAllister (10)	101
Liam Sharrock (9)	102
Cara Wishart (8)	103
Sarah Jepson (9)	103
Georgia Richardson (8)	104
Daniel McDonald (10)	104
Sophie Davies (9)	105

St Joseph's RC Primary School, Heywood

Thomas Croly (11)	105
Laura Hutchinson (10)	106
Jade Mullen (10)	106
Darren Parker (11)	107
Christopher Wroe (11)	107
Catherine Keane (11)	108
Aaron Brown (11)	108
Rebecca Butler (10)	109
Dominic Briddon (10)	109
Dean Smith (11)	110
Chenise Fulton (11)	110
Nathan McGuinness (11)	111
Daniel Fleming (10)	111
Lauren Bond (11)	112
Bethany Krauza (11)	112
Chantelle McDowall (11)	113
Gregory Weir (11)	113
Sophie Crewe (11)	114
Amy Davenport (11)	114
Natalie Duffy (11)	115
Grace Murphy (11)	115
Suzanne Blyzniuk (11)	116
Thomas McGeown (11)	116
Callum Murphy (11)	117
Ryan Dolan (11)	117
Emily Peplow (11)	117
Katie Beese (11)	118

Katie Imrie (11)	132
Laura Anton (10)	132
Travis Noblett (11)	132
Andrew Tierney (11)	133
Lee Holt (11)	133
Jordan Murphy (10)	133
Kelly Wallwork (10)	134
Emily Hargreaves (11)	134
Liam Delaney (10)	135
Lindsey Flux (11)	135
Danny Mercer (11)	135
Jamie Goodman (10)	136
Samuel Fishwick (10)	136
Oliver Lee (11)	136
Danielle Troake (11)	137
Alexander Straw (10)	137
Ruth Evans (10)	137
Ania Neisser (11)	138
Charlotte Flanagan (9)	138
Matthew Wilson (11)	139
Jessica Clitheroe (11)	139
Helena Kelly (8)	139
Catherine Richardson (11)	140
Katie Farley (9)	140
Daniel Forshaw (8)	140
Joseph Ellison (8)	141
Danny Harty (9)	141
Scott Whittle (10)	141
Poppy Aldridge (10)	142
Rebecca Linfitt (8)	142
Sam Wright (10)	143
Vikki Bowler (9)	143
Euan Dickson (11)	144

St Mary's Hall School, Stonyhurst

Thomas Holden (11)	144
Edward Courteney-Harris (11)	144
Alexander Ahmed (10)	145
Joshua Vines (11)	145
James Gale (11)	146
Grace Mercer (8)	146

St Patrick's School, Rochdale

Heather Pye (7)   189
Matthew Swinburne (7)   189

Sacred Heart RC Primary School
Grace Feehan (9)   189
Ciaran Gannon (9)   190
Elizabeth Robinson (9)   190
Ella Ogden (8)   190
Chloe Roscoe (9)   191
Zacharia Jordan Kaye (8)   191
Harry Kaye (8)   191
Mellisa Hind (9)   192
Molly Frankland (9)   192
Connor Hennessy-King (9)   192
Fintan Rowan Young (8)   193
Yasmin Bracewell (9)   193
Jessica Ayers (9)   193
Shaun McArdle-Watson (8)   194
Harry Kavanagh (8)   194
Rachel Curran (9)   195
Alex Bailey (9)   195

Sherwood Primary School
Georgina Abram (11)   195
Sameera Auckburally (10)   196
Emily Bradley (11)   196
Charlotte Bamber (11)   197
Laurie Cameron (9)   197
Mary Clayton (11)   198
Francesca Deaville (11)   198
Emma Cook (10)   199
Emily Kay (11)   199
Daniel Duckworth (11)   199
Rebecca Fisher (10)   200
Peter Gawne (11)   200
Mohammed Mitha (11)   200
Kate Jefferies (11)   201
Rabia Khan (11)   201
Oliver Nelson (10)   201
Tara-Jo Leyland (11)   202
Dalton Riley (10)   202

Jenny Mortlock (11)	203
Jade Pike (11)	203
Joseph Nithsdale (11)	204
Melissa Pang (11)	204
Bethany Leeming (10)	204
Rachel Wood (11)	205
Rachel Tate (10)	205
Mark Tate (10)	206
Holly Pears (11)	206
Duncan Young (10)	206
Jennifer Reilly (10)	207

Whalley CE Primary School
Emily Trickett (9)	207
Sam Wells (8)	208
Megan Jackson (9)	208
Kelly Mashiter (8)	209
Sylvie Bowman (8)	209
Olivia Jackson (11)	210
Jessica Wild (9)	211
William Lancaster (8)	212

Wray-With-Botton Endowed School
Ben Wallbank (8)	212
John Staveley (8)	212
Joe Atkinson (9)	213
Robert Staveley (11)	213
Esther Preece (10)	214
Tamsin Seed (9)	214
Lois Preece (8)	215
Lily Hughes (11)	216
Virginia Hartley (10)	216

The Poems

School Fights

School fights are very dangerous
And sometimes they're pointless.

School fights have punching and kicking,
I know a boy who can't stop spitting.

School fights have calling and crying,
So the teacher says, 'Stop fighting.'

But the boys keep on hitting,
Then comes the boy who is very rough,
So then he starts acting tough,
Then the teacher says, 'Stop that fight, Buff.'

'OK Miss, all done now.'
But then goes a pow!
So then the fight starts all over again.

Matthew Anderton (9)
Bedford Hall Methodist Primary School

In The Jungle Overseas

In the jungle overseas
I saw monkeys swinging in trees

In the jungle overseas
I saw giraffes with knobbly knees

In the jungle overseas
I saw ants collecting leaves

In the jungle overseas
I saw flowers, I saw bees

In the jungle overseas
I saw tigers eating my keys

In the jungle overseas
I saw lions chasing *me!*

Matthew Skivington (8)
Bedford Hall Methodist Primary School

At The Beach

I saw a horse and some dogs
When I went to the beach

I saw a starfish and some crabs
When I went to the beach

I saw a rock pool and sea monkeys
When I went to the beach

I saw a seagull on a sandcastle
When I went to the beach

I saw a speedboat bobbing along
When I went to the beach

I saw a pelican and some sharks
When I went to the beach

I saw a stingray and some jellyfish
When I went to the beach

I saw a hammerhead shark and some seaweed
When I went to the beach

I saw a man selling doughnuts and ice cream
When I went to the beach

I saw a hang-glider flying along
When I went to the beach.

Jessica Eccles (8)
Bedford Hall Methodist Primary School

My Dog

My dog likes dog food,
It gives him a mood,
He goes for walks,
He comes off his lead,
It makes him tough,
It keeps him warm.

Adil Anderson (9)
Bedford Hall Methodist Primary School

The Sunny Beach

One day at the beach,
I was eating a peach.

When we arrived we
Found a beehive.

The coffee machine broke
And my sister choked.

I had loads of fun,
Drinking in the sun.

We ran to the fair,
We called our friend Buffy Bear.

We had loads of showers,
While we were looking at flowers.

The showers were falling,
While we were calling.

Our friend who's a baby needed a nappy,
But I was playing and I was happy.

Kirsty Aiello (8)
Bedford Hall Methodist Primary School

Down In The Jungle

Down in the jungle where the lions live
They all go roar, roar, *roar!*
Down in the jungle where the monkeys live
They all go ee, ee, *ee!*
Down in the jungle where the gorillas live
They all go boom, boom, *boom!*
Down in the jungle where the giraffes live
They all go chomp, chomp, *chomp!*
Down in the jungle where the people live
They all go bang, bang, *bang!*

Sophie Stephens (8)
Bedford Hall Methodist Primary School

All In My Own Backyard

Staring at the stars
Spying at Mars
All in my own backyard

Having a bit of fun
Falling and calling for Mum
All in my own backyard

But Mum's minding Mark!
I can't get up because it's too dark,
All in my own backyard

I call Mum out
She starts to shout
All in my own backyard.

Lucy Barton (8)
Bedford Hall Methodist Primary School

I Hope My School Is . . .

I hope my school is colourful
And all the teachers are wonderful
I want my friends to care for me
As good as they can be

I hope my school is clean
And no one is mean
People don't shout
Until school's out

I hope the children are polite
And never ever fight
When the day is over I see the light
Shining ever so bright.

Bethany Gregory (9)
Bedford Hall Methodist Primary School

Inside My School

Teacher, teacher
I didn't mean to
I'm late again
What should I do?

My writing, my reading
Or even my maths
I do like PE and RE
Even going to the baths

Sometimes I think school is cool
Sometimes I think school is cruel

On a Friday
School is the best
We get to do PE, art and maths

On a Monday
School is good
Because I do PE
Maths and geography too!

On a Tuesday
School is cruel
Because I do no good lessons
In school.

Kelsey Hackett (9)
Bedford Hall Methodist Primary School

My Friends

The thing I like best is playing out
I tell some jokes
I play some games
I sometimes see a plane
When I play with my friends
My mum sends me
To the shop.

Thomas Hampson (8)
Bedford Hall Methodist Primary School

My Cat, Lewis

My cat, Lewis
Sleeps most of
The day

My cat, Lewis
Wakes up and
Expects food on
Her tray

My cat, Lewis
I got in
May

I took her
Home and on
The settee
She lay

Quiet and gentle
I tiptoe around
Without making
A sound

I love my
Cat Lewis
She's gorgeous
And fluffy

Before she goes to bed
I make sure her
Pillow's puffy.

Shannon Lee (9)
Bedford Hall Methodist Primary School

Things Are Always Missing

Work is always disappearing
In a few days it's reappearing
They put it in their folder
While the talking gets bolder

Paper, pencils and pens,
All end up in their dens,
Pencils are flinging,
While the bell is ringing
And the teacher comes into our sight.

She's holding her bag
And she sees all the pens,
The pencils on her desk
And all the classroom dens.

Paper, pencils and pens,
All end up in their dens,
Pencils are flinging,
While the bell is ringing
And the teacher walks into our sight.

Michael Walters (10)
Bedford Hall Methodist Primary School

The Wounded World

If you don't care,
No one else will,
All there will be left is a little pear,
Everyone will have to take a pill,
Because everyone will be very ill,
So please look after the world.

Frances Roberts (9)
Bedford Hall Methodist Primary School

Classroom Rap

Sorry I am late but my
Mum could not clean the plate
She stayed in bed and I
Thought she was dead

'I hope you're not late tomorrow,'
Said the teacher
'I am sorry, I will not be late tomorrow,'
I replied

There I am sat at my table
Now comes the teacher holding a book
And reading a fable

Yes, yes, it is art today
And I think art is the best
And I also like ICT
But I really don't like RE.

Aaron Brown (10)
Bedford Hall Methodist Primary School

A Hot Sunny Day

I'm sat on the beach,
Eating a peach,
I'm sat on the sand,
Watching a band.

I'm singing a song,
Walking along.
I'm combing my hair,
Watching the fair.

I'm sat in the sun,
Having some fun,
When Mum calls me in,
To empty the bin.

Rebecca Unsworth (9)
Bedford Hall Methodist Primary School

School Days

Here I am, I'm sat in the middle
Oh no, I'm starting to giggle

Here comes the teacher
I'm in for it now
Have you got your spelling book
No Miss, I've lost it

Here I am in the hall
Chucking a small round ball
Smash! Goes a window
What can I do?
Stay in after school and pay for that window

Here I am, I am tucked up in bed
Dreading what will happen tomorrow
I close my eyes and dream what a horrible day I've had.

Matthew Gardner (10)
Bedford Hall Methodist Primary School

I Hate School!

I hate school,
I don't think it's cool,
Geography is bad,
But RE is the worst.

Literacy is good,
But maths is better,
It don't change my decision.

I think art's wicked,
But games is 100% cool.

Summer holidays I like best,
Because no school means no work

And that is why I hate school,
So live with it.

Myles Hindley (10)
Bedford Hall Methodist Primary School

Oh No!

In my class I've got some friends
Who are quite strange
But are fun and games
We have such fun
We roam, we play
We jump and bounce
We talk all day

Now Dean my mate
He's small but clever
He's always talking to
Girls and fellas

Oh yeah that Reece
He's very nosy
He's always poking into
Others' business
He can't keep quiet
For over a minute

Now the girls
Danielle's so funny
She's my best mate at school
And doesn't like running

Now Kelsey, she's always cheeky
And is always laughing
But mostly chatting
Yesterday she got busted
I think Mrs Dickman wanted to throw
Her in the dustbin

So now you know
That in my class I have some friends
Who are quite strange
But there are fun and games
We have such fun
We roam and play
We jump and bounce
We talk all day.

Samantha Dobson (10)
Bedford Hall Methodist Primary School

Excuses When You're Late

Sorry I'm late
My mum was ill
She keeps moaning
About Uncle Bill

Sorry I'm late
My sister stayed in bed
My mum thought
She was dead

Sorry I'm late
I've had no food
And my sister thinks
I'm very crude

Sorry I'm late
My puppy died
So my mum and sister
Cried, cried, cried

Sorry I'm late
A rat was in my house
Then it turned out
To be a mouse

Sorry I'm late
My mum couldn't drop me off
Because she has
A really bad cough

Sorry I'm late
My sister was sick
All over my mum's boyfriend
Who's called Nick.

John Gilman (10)
Bedford Hall Methodist Primary School

Classroom Mayhem

Reece is like Pinocchio,
His nose is rather long,
At the end of Wednesday, it's music,
We like to have a sing-song.

On Thursday we go to the baths,
We go to swim and laugh,
Reece thinks he swims,
But at the pool, he got pushed in.

I like school,
It's rather cool,
The best part
Is when we do art.

We do RE
And PE,
They're rather fun
And very good

Kelsey and Sammy D
Are my two best friends,
My other friends are funny,
But Kelsey and Sammy D are simply the best!

I like school,
It's rather cool,
The best part
Is when we do art.

Danielle Skivington (10)
Bedford Hall Methodist Primary School

Brett Lost His Pen

This afternoon Brett lost his pen,
He tells the teacher,
The teacher says, 'Go away.'
He looks around the class,
He finds his pen, it never lasts.

The day after, he gets a new pen,
He loses it again!
On Tuesday he goes hurrying to Miss Lane,
Brett says, 'I need a new pen.'
Miss Lane says, 'Go away.'
He goes hurrying to the teacher.

She gives him a new pen,
With string on it,
He never lost it again,
As it was wrapped round his neck!

Jasmine Steward (9)
Bedford Hall Methodist Primary School

Classroom Rap

Have you got your brains ready?
Because this is the classroom rap

Sorry I was late
For my mum couldn't pass the gate
She stayed in bed
But I said,
'C'mon Mum, it's time for school
There's no time for the pool'

Sorry I'm late
I couldn't catch a bus
Because they said no under-11s on this bus
And my mum
Well, let's just say
That she is ill.

Jordan Tomlinson (10)
Bedford Hall Methodist Primary School

In Our School

In school we do everything
And when we go in the hall
We always sing

Sometimes I don't like school
Sometimes I think it's cool

First, we do our maths
And then we go to the baths

At the big hall
We always have to sing
And always sit up very tall

We do literacy
We do geography
We do RE
We do PE

If I am stuck on my work
I ask the teacher for some help

I am sometimes late
I am sometimes early
But this morning my mum had a tummy ache

Sometimes there's a mouse
Inside my big huge house.

Christopher Yates (10)
Bedford Hall Methodist Primary School

In Jamaica

In Jamaica
Under the sea
They're selling fish
Small ones, big ones
Take your pick
It all depends
On your son, Nick.

Johnathan Eckersley (11)
Bedford Hall Methodist Primary School

The Seaside's Beauty

The cry of the seagull
The breeze off the sea
The salty taste of fish and chips
Over the road from you and me

The beautiful sea with waves
Bobbing up and down
The children's laughter all the way in town

Buckets and spades thrown everywhere
I ask my mum if I can have an ice cream
From the van over there

The cry of the seagull
The breeze off the sea
The salty taste of fish and chips
Over the road from you and me.

Lucy Aubrey-Snow (11)
Bedford Hall Methodist Primary School

My Cat

My cat,
Likes to play on the mat.

She sleeps all day
And gets her own way.

She rolls in dirt,
Then on my shirt.

She likes to chase string,
When I'm on the swing.

She hides under the bed,
Waiting to be fed.

She brings birds in the house,
But I've never found a mouse.

She lies in the road to stop the cars,
One day she'll end up behind bars.

Demi Leather (10)
Bedford Hall Methodist Primary School

The Zoo

Once upon a time,
I went to the zoo,
I saw a big, fat, ugly tiger
That doubled into two!

I saw a six foot snake
Staring up at me,
One minute it was there, and then
It trebled into three!

A monkey was eating lots of bananas,
It wanted more and more,
Stupid, fat monkey, *wow!*
It quadrupled into four!

A giraffe was being very boring,
It looked barely alive,
It was lying down in peace,
Until there were five!

Once upon a time, I left a zoo,
Someone threw a ball at me,
'Argh, you are so stupid!'
I trebled into three!

Jake Barnes (11)
Bedford Hall Methodist Primary School

In The Deep Dark Woods

I saw a fox with some socks
In the deep dark woods

I saw a wolf and a gull
In the deep dark woods

I saw a tumbled-down cottage
In the deep dark woods

I heard a wolf behind a tree
In the deep dark woods.

Jessica Clay (8)
Bedford Hall Methodist Primary School

Visit To My Grandad

When I'm with Grandad
He treats me like gold,
He acts like a monkey
He's never really bold.

We play in the park
Together me and him,
We have our own world
Not much anymore, he loves that fat lady Kim.

When I'm with my grandad
We are a pair,
I think my mum is jealous
She says it's not fair.

I love my grandad really bad
I know he loves me too,
We are like animals
Parading through the zoo.

I love my grandad lots and lots
Forever we will play,
I'll always love my grandad
Whatever people say!

Keeley Berry (11)
Bedford Hall Methodist Primary School

Flowers

Lovely flowers bloom
From April until July
On clematis plants

Some plants bloom again
Later in the year in Fall
Lightening the heart

Roses are pretty
Busy lizzies are so few
All flowers are lovely.

Charlotte Stout (10)
Bedford Hall Methodist Primary School

My Gran Thinks She's A Rock Star!

My gran acts like she's twenty-two,
She has sky-blue hair,
She always listens to heavy metal,
What a nightmare!

She dresses in baggy jeans,
Even though she's sixty-nine,
In chains and skulls,
I can't believe this gran is mine!

She loves Eminem,
She never turns her stereo down,
It's giving me a headache,
It's driving me round and round!

One day I went to her house,
She pretended to be a rock star,
I never want to listen to heavy metal again,
Not one electric guitar!

That day I turned 'Meatloaf' off
And told her to give it a rest,
She turned round and said to me,
'Look love, I'm simply the best!'

No matter how hard I try,
She'll not turn her music off,
She'll keep acting like she's twenty-two,
Even though she's not!

Amy Barton (11)
Bedford Hall Methodist Primary School

My New Car

On Monday I looked all day,
I looked all day for a car,
Finally I looked no more,
I found my perfect car.

On Tuesday I picked up my new car,
The first thing I did was fill it full of petrol,
The second thing I did was drive, drive, drive,
Until I could drive no more.

On Wednesday I put a bit of petrol in and
Bang!
I blew up the engine,
So I rang the AA to give me a hand.

On Thursday I tried to fix it,
But I couldn't,
I gave my mate John a call to give me a tow,
But once we'd got to the garage, *pop!*

On Friday,
We tried to repair the tyre after running into a nail,
I said to him,
'You might as well put a new set of tyres on the bill,
I mean, I'm already paying for a new engine.'

On Saturday,
My new car came out of the garage,
With new wheels and engine,
Once I'd paid off the debt, I was back on the road.

On Sunday, I filled my car full of petrol,
Then I went 60 in a 20 mph zone,
Once I paid off the £200 bill I . . .
Crash!
Oh, here we go again.

Alistair Mills (11)
Bedford Hall Methodist Primary School

Once Upon A Rhyme

Down beside the seaside
Lives a funny girl called Rose
The most disgusting thing she does
Is she always picks her nose

Down beside the seaside
Lives a girl called Kelly
The funniest thing about her
Is she's always called smelly

Down beside the seaside
Lives a naughty boy called Caine
The thing his mother hates about him
Is he's always being a pain

Down beside the seaside
Lives a boy called Zack
The most silly thing about him
Is he can't look back

Down beside the seaside
Lives a silly girl called Sue
The most silly thing about her
Is she's always on the loo

Down beside the seaside
Lives a boy called Eddie
The most funny thing about him
Is he's always called Freddie.

Kimberley Hilton (11)
Bedford Hall Methodist Primary School

Green

Green is like apples
that are nice to eat

Green is like a leaf
that falls from the trees

Green is like mould
that grows on bread

Green is the colour
of my uniform

Green is like grass
I like to play on it

Green is a felt tip pen
I colour things in with it

Green is a pear
Nice and delicious to eat

Green is grape juice
Nice and refreshing to drink.

Jordan Sanders (11)
Bedford Hall Methodist Primary School

I Don't Like School

Today I'm going to school,
But I just sat on my stool,
I explained how the teachers were cruel,
They won't let me dive in the pool,
My friends are nasty,
Blaming everything on me,
They run off when we play tig,
They always scare me with earwigs,
The food is horrible,
The cook is terrible,
I got off my stool
And shouted, 'I don't like school!'

Louise Chan (9)
Bedford Hall Methodist Primary School

Orange

Orange is like the sun,
giving us all light.

Orange is like a leaf,
in autumn on the ground.

Orange is like the juice,
that you gulp down your throat.

Orange is like a goldfish,
that wiggles its tail all day.

Orange is like an octopus,
with many waving legs.

Orange is like a balloon,
that goes up until it pops.

Orange is like a flower,
growing in the sun.

Orange is like a fire,
giving us all heat.

Orange is like a crayon,
that we colour with.

Orange is like an orange,
as juicy as could be.

Lindsay Miller (11)
Bedford Hall Methodist Primary School

The Snake

The snake is very slippery,
It slithers along the path . . .
Until it sees a tall giraffe!

The giraffe is too tall for my dinner,
I will go and find something thinner!

Laura Oldfield (6)
Catforth Primary School

Shopping

Shopping is what I do
Are you like that too?
I keep the bags
Throw the tags
And show the stuff off to my cousin, Mags
Shopping for me is a mega addiction
My cousin says it's all just fiction
I like the way I shop and dress
Not like my cousin who's a bit of a mess
I love to shop and
Buy a new designer top
I like earrings on my ears
I want to look like Britney Spears
I saw a skirt
And a matching shirt
Or what about that red T-shirt?
Mags is just fashionless
Now I've got to sort out her sister, Tess
And who knows
What's next?

Gabriella Giannoccaro (10)
Catforth Primary School

I Want To Taste

I want to taste
A punnet of strawberries
Sneaking out of the fridge
Into the thick foaming cream

I want to taste
Sausages sneaking out of the oven door
Into the thick brown sauce

I want to taste
Garlic gliding around the oven door
Guarding it.

Kieran Hamilton (9)
Catforth Primary School

Mysterious Fruit

It's round and juicy
And very fruity

It's red and green
It makes you quite lean

I like it cold in the sun
I shoot the pips with a pellet gun

It's lovely for your lunch
When you bite into it, it goes *crunch!*

It's the best fruit ever
I'll love it forever

It makes a sticky mess
Can you guess?

Ashleigh Butler (10)
Catforth Primary School

My Cat

I love my cat
He's fat and furry
Nice and smooth
His colour is black and white
My cat is sometimes a fool
He dances around and drools
He loves getting cuddled
Most of the time he is taking it cool
Relaxing on the sofa
But he is too big to pick up and cuddle
He weighs 18 pounds
So he is always easy to find!

Ian Terrell (11)
Catforth Primary School

Mystery Man

He's got long, lanky legs
And big black boots
He's a mystery man
Who drives a white van

He creeps into a house
As silent as a mouse
He's a lean, mean man
And I hate him so

It's very frightening
A bit like lightning
The dark sky covers the whole earth . . .
The mystery man worries me.

Kathy Stones (9)
Catforth Primary School

Food

I like my food sweet
I like chocolate
It's the best

I like fish
In a dish

I like cake
When it's freshly made

I like chips
Freshly made
With tomato sauce.

Emily Terrell (8)
Catforth Primary School

I Wish, I Wish

I wish I was so tiny to see the bugs and make friends
I wish I had some super cool spy glasses with X-ray lenses
I wish I was the boss to say what's what
I wish I had a school of rock
I wish I was a rabbit to run around in a hurry
I wish I had a magic cloth to wipe away my worries
I wish I had a mind like a calculator to test the teacher's brains
I wish I felt no pain
I wish my mum would shut up about fuss
I wish I was a superhero to take off with the birds
I wish I was the king, to be very important
I wish I was rich enough to buy anything I wanted
But at the end of the day I just want to snuggle up in bed.

Jacob Odix (10)
Catforth Primary School

My Bed

I don't really like my bed at night,
It's not that I'm scared of the monsters that would give me a fright.

It's because I can never get to sleep,
All I want to do is get up and peep.

Sometimes my dad shouts really loud,
It's like he thinks that I'm in a crowd

And sometimes I go to bed late,
So Mum shouts, 'You better get to sleep mate.'

I'm never really that dozy,
But if I am I'll snuggle down cosy.

Harriet Parkinson (10)
Catforth Primary School

My Pet

I have a pet rabbit
She can be naughty but she's also rather sweet
She runs about in her fluffy coat
And she's really, really neat

I have a pet dog
He's really well trained
He's soft and cuddly too
He can be bad
It can make me sad
When I wash him he looks as good as new

I have a pet pig
She's very short and does everything she's taught
She waddles about
And sniffs with her snout
And sometimes I have to *shout*

I have a pet parrot
Whose name is Billy
He's very silly
He copies everything
He flaps his wing and tries to sing.

Nicola Birch (8)
Catforth Primary School

I Like . . .

I like the taste of greasy sausages that have been cooked in the oven,
I like the taste of garlic bread making my mouth water as it
                              comes out of the oven,
I like the taste of slippery, slimy, swirly spaghetti,
I like the taste of chips, all crunchy and soft,
I like the taste of milk, cold and fresh - just come out of the fridge,
I like the taste of chocolate, all runny and white,
But most of all I like
Sweets!

Connor Hardie (9)
Catforth Primary School

I Keep

I keep . . .
10 kittens, small and fluffy,
9 dogs, big and strong,
8 ducks that quack all night,
7 kangaroos that bounce all the way,
6 snakes that coil round the legs of my bed,
5 fish that swim all day,
4 hippos, dirty and messy,
3 cheeky monkeys that swing from vines,
2 flamingos, tall and straight and
1 elephant, huge and fat.
No wonder my room is so messy, don't blame me!

Alexandra Butcher (9)
Catforth Primary School

Steve's Pets

In his bedroom Steve kept . . .
Ten ants that are his leftovers
Nine flies that dirtied his room
Eight spiders that were after the flies
Seven tarantulas that snuggled into bed
Six lizards that crept on his head
Five snakes that slithered slippery on the floor
Four cats that jumped on the door
Three dogs that barked at night
Two wasps that gave a fright
And one - guess what?

Harry Rose (9)
Catforth Primary School

The Flamingo

Hello, I am a flamingo
My friends call me Flimy

I fly through the jungle
My colour is pink and I am skinny

I am so bright
But I never show up in the night

When I eat I get fuller
And my friends love my colour.

Beth Odix (7)
Catforth Primary School

Monster Attack

There once was a monster
Whose claws tore doors
His slimy, slithering serpents
Came through the floors

He ate hounds
And lived underground
When he's happy he goes
Round and round

He bashed people
On the head
And clashed people
Against the walls

He balanced beds
On his heads
He went to bed
With a load of teds

He's very hairy
On the chest
So he wears
Lots of vests!

Rachael Murby (9)
Caton Community Primary School

The Dog That Saved The World

The dog saved the world today,
So please don't fret,
This dog will come your way,
No need for the vet.

Help! Help the dog!
Help! Help me!
Help! Help the frog!
Help! Help the sight to see!
The dog that saved the world.

Doggie, there's no time to dig,
No time to learn to dive,
No time to even chuck a twig,
Now come on, let's dive!

Help! Help the dog!
Help! Help me!
Help! Help the frog!
Help! Help the sight to see!
The dog that saved the world.

Well now he's saved the world,
He is soooo sweet!
He has saved the mountains curled,
Now he deserves his meat.

Please thank the dog,
Please thank me,
Please thank the frog,
Please thank the sight to see,
The dog that saved the world!

Kathryn Mills (10)
Caton Community Primary School

The Lunch Box To Make You Scream!

There goes the bell
And look the clock's just chimed,
Oh look, oh help,
It's dreaded dinner time!

I walk to the coat pegs,
Get my lunch box and run,
It's trying to bite my fingers off,
There's no hope for eating a bun.

There goes the bell
And look the clock's just chimed,
Oh look, oh help,
It's dreaded dinner time.

It's got a frowning face
And a sneering grin,
I wish I could and I can,
Stick it in the bin.

There goes the bell
And look the clock's just chimed,
Oh look, oh help,
It's dreaded dinner time.

I wish Mum would buy me a new one!

Ella Jarman (9)
Caton Community Primary School

Pets

I have a dog, his name is Patch,
He is very cuddly,
But he does scratch.

He has big paws,
Which are good to catch,
But even though he does snatch.

Stacy Brown (9)
Caton Community Primary School

I Hate Hurricanes!

I hate hurricanes,
The lightning is frightening,
The rushing of rain,
I hate hurricanes.

I hate hurricanes,
The covering clouds,
The terrifying thunder,
I hate hurricanes.

I hate hurricanes,
The flowing of the rivers,
Across the streets,
I hate hurricanes.

Emma Hodgson (10)
Caton Community Primary School

Older Sisters

O lder sisters are a pain
L azy and lousy
D oubtful and bossy
E very time you speak they shout
R ebecca is one of those sisters

S aying stuff you don't understand
I can't take it anymore
S isters are a real bore
T elling you off
E very day
R owdy, moody sisters
S o why don't I run away?

Katie Harding (10)
Caton Community Primary School

The Car

I was driving down the motorway
In a McLaren F1
Then an Alfa Romeo Tipo 33 Stradale
Came zooming past us like a bullet from a gun

I tried to catch it with my foot on the floor
But still needed a little bit more
And all I could see was a cloud of dust
From a Volvo C70

I continued on my way
On a big long motorway
I was just about to turn off
When I saw the Alfa Romeo Tipo 33 Stradale
Broken down on the hard shoulder
I finally passed it!

Oliver Parsons (10)
Caton Community Primary School

Poem

The whistle blows
Leonard passes with pace
It goes to a defender
Who has a lot of space

The defender smacks the ball
It lands in the box
Where Leonard is stood
He is as sly as a fox

Just on 89 minutes
The manager was having a fret
Leonard kicked the ball
And it was in the net.

Ryan Leonard (9)
Caton Community Primary School

The School To Make You Scream!

Just off the edge of the world,
There is a school
In the big school there is a curved room
Do worry it's the school to make you scream!

In the school there is a broom
It's filled with nasty potions and antidotes
In the broom is a picture of a room
In the picture of a room is a boat

Just off the edge of the world
There is a school
In the big school there is a curved room
Do worry it's the school to make you scream!

In the school there is a cupboard
In the cupboard there is a broom
It's the broom from verse one
Argh! See, it made you scream.

Just off the edge of the world,
There is a school,
In the big school there is a curved room,
Do worry it's the school to make you scream!

Sarah Murby (10)
Caton Community Primary School

My Teacher

My teacher's called Mrs Brown,
She's the funniest teacher ever,
We always play a game of rounders,
It doesn't matter about the weather.

My teacher's called Mrs Brown,
She wears a pen in her hair,
She's so good and fantastic,
She's so very, very rare.

Amy France (9)
Caton Community Primary School

Aircraft Time Line Poem

1903,
Orville and Wilbur Wright,
In their home-made flyer,
Flew the first flight.

1914,
The Fokker Triplaned Hun,
Our Sopwith Camels,
Shot him down with a gun.

1939,
In comes the Spit,
Shoot down a Nazi
In his Messerschmitt.

1941
And the Lancaster,
Lots more planes,
Can go even faster.

The 1990s,
The Hawk scaring sparrows,
The red variations
Used by The Red Arrows.

1991,
The Tornado that's tan,
It's really cool,
With a huge wingspan.

2000+,
Hypersoar,
Skipping in space,
Slowness in planes no more!

David Riley (10)
Caton Community Primary School

Spring Animals

In the field with green grass,
Horses' hooves pounding the ground
Ducks with ducklings
A baby bunny is what I've found

Five in the field
Cows moo
Sheep baa, baa
I wish I could too

In the field with green grass
Horses' hooves pounding the ground
Ducks with ducklings
A baby lamb is what I've found

Ponies neighing
Cows eating
Sheep are lying down
Lambs' hearts are beating

In the field with green grass
Horses' hooves pounding the ground
Ducks with ducklings
A baby pony is what I've found

Imagine a field without any of them
No head peeking through the fence
No bunnies, no cows
What nonsense!

Samantha Haggan (9)
Caton Community Primary School

Alphabet Poem

A my the alligator likes acting,
B en the bat brings burgers to the bullrings,
C alum the crab likes catching,
D avid the dinosaur likes discos,
E llie the elephant will be eating,
F reddy the ferret likes singing songs,
G eorge the giraffe likes to pong,
H enry the horse likes jumping,
I ssy the insect likes bumping,
J anet the jellyfish likes jokes
K aty the kitten likes notes
L ia the lion likes coats
M olly the monkey likes lions
N orma the newt likes the moon
O lly the owl likes the afternoon
P oppy the puffer likes having pigtails
Q ueen the quail likes boat sails
R obert the robot likes oil
S ammy the snake likes foil
T ony the turtle likes you
U ri the umbrella likes Lou
V inny the vixen likes violins
W illiam the whale likes mandarins
X -ery the ox likes losing
Y olly the yak likes music
Z olly the zebra likes *zzzzz!*

Alicia Clegg (7)
Christ Church CE Primary School

Vampire Bat

One day a surprise happened,
My big brother turned into a vampire bat,
He now has fangs,
And a taste for blood,
But he still has long hair.

He found he had wings
And that he could fly,
So he flew up into the sky.

When he got old,
He became blind,
But he still isn't very kind.

He made up his own song
And it goes like this,
'I come out at night
To suck your blood,
I come through your window
At twelve o'clock,
I'm out of control
And I hate pest control
Because they put me in Chester Zoo!'

Elliot Howley (9)
Christ Church CE Primary School

My Rose Bush

I went outside and saw my roses
Pink, red and white
Look at the colourful sight
They need the light
They took ages to grow
I always stop to say, 'Hello'
In the wind they said '*Ssssh.'*

Robyn Warrington (8)
Christ Church CE Primary School

I Wanna Be . . .

I wanna be a chocolate
Nice, bold and sweet
That would be a treat!

I wanna be a flower
Made out of solid gold
To be looked at and admired
And be eventually sold!

I wanna be a worm
Wiggling through the holes
Meeting up with spiders and moles!

I wanna be a mountain
Big, huge and steep
It's better than being deep

I wanna be a rainforest
Fresh, green and free
That will be absolutely me!

Wait a minute . . .
I just wanna be
Me!

Heather Johnson (11)
Christ Church CE Primary School

My Dog

Although he is small,
He can fetch a ball
And the hole he can dig
Is ever so big,
When he buries his bone,
The grown-ups, they moan,
Because he has dug up the shed instead!

Matthew Byrom (7)
Christ Church CE Primary School

My Dad

My dad has a goatee beard,
Sometimes he is nice,
Without his glasses everything looks smeared,
It's weird but my dad hates mice.

He taught me how to swim,
He helps me with my maths,
I suppose you could say he's kinda slim,
After walking all those paths.

When he walks round he brings his pong,
He buys lots of games,
Sometimes my dad is wrong
And he calls me some funny names.

My dad plays his guitar,
Sometimes he does shout,
He's my number one dad by far,
But sometimes I wish he'd keep his nose out.

Emily Duthie (9)
Christ Church CE Primary School

My Special Friend

My special friend
Has lots of toys
She hangs around with boys
Emma is funny
She has lots of money
She wears skirts
And always wears T-shirts
She is very pretty
No wonder it's a pity
Emma is very kind
She's the only one who I can find.

Aimee Mahoney (8)
Christ Church CE Primary School

I Am My Dog!

I would like to be my dog,
To climb upon a log,
Cos she is so small
And I am not very tall.

She is very strong
And I am not very long,
I wished upon God,
To turn me into a dog.

The next thing I knew,
I went up and flew,
When I came back down,
I turned round and round.

I was so small,
Everything was tall,
I was a dog,
I can climb on a log!

Holly Espie (11)
Christ Church CE Primary School

My Brother

I am an annoying little wind up,
My brother knows it's true,
I always get him in trouble for things he doesn't do.

I act like I'm the good one
And he is just a pest,
I tell everyone his secrets
About his bright pink vest.

But today it is his birthday,
So guess what his present is?
A handful of wind-ups from
Me, his favourite sis.

Jodie Anchor (9)
Christ Church CE Primary School

It's My Turn!

It's my turn to count
I'm going to get you on
Because I'm not going to recount
It won't take me very long
I'm walking around the corner
I think I can see
My best friend Peter up the tree
A pile of leaves I can see
I see a red shirt, who can it be?
It must be Holly
Wearing her LFC
I walk quite far
I hear a car
I must be near a road
Now it's time to go home.

Sam Reynolds (11)
Christ Church CE Primary School

Found You

'Ready or not, here I am'
Everything was still until someone ran
Everything was still and quiet again
I looked in the shed for clues
What did I see? Two shoes
'Found you!'
Or have I?
I look further and further,
Until I have found . . .
What is that poking out of the ground?
Shall I go closer to see, but if I do,
Someone will jump out and say
'I got you!'

Robert McLintock (11)
Christ Church CE Primary School

I Would Like To Be A Flower

Oh how I wish to be a flower,
If someone had such power,
Gazing up to the sun,
Oh it would be such fun.

I would be red,
In a flowerbed,
Or a daisy,
Being lazy.

Maybe a poppy,
But everyone would copy,
It's so easy
But a bit breezy.

So now I think -
I'm being a fruit,
Yes, I think that
Would suit.

Rebecca Connell (11)
Christ Church CE Primary School

I Am A Unicorn

I turned into a unicorn,
Then I found out I could fly,
Away up in the sky,
I had lilac wings,
I felt like I was on springs.

I had a silky, golden mane,
Unicorns should be trained,
But I somehow trained myself,
I also had a golden tail,
I love to follow my silver trail.

Frances Taylor (9)
Christ Church CE Primary School

My Brother

Have you ever heard of my brother, Michael?
He's always bossing me around
One day I decided to get my own back
I got a microchip from my drawer
And stuck it in his drinking straw

He swallowed it down, it gurgled in his tummy
He started complaining, 'Oh it hurts me Mummy'
I sat behind the sofa laughing and giggling
It went down smoothly - without any jiggling

The next day I got up early and started to control him
When he was dressed, I controlled him to the shop
He got some sweets but that was the end of him
And the invention of the servant brother.

Why don't you try it?

Rachel Coope (10)
Christ Church CE Primary School

The Wind's Secrets

If you hear the wind whispering in your ear,
Don't turn back and run away, don't show it your fear,
Stay . . . sit down . . . and listen,
For the wind is telling you its secrets.

He tells you about the fairies,
Dancing in the forest,
The butterflies and their golden wings,
The birds that sing the sweetest song,
While flying past the pink and purple meadows,
All day long, please sit and listen, for the wind
Is telling you its secret.

Lauren Warrington (10)
Christ Church CE Primary School

Pink Blossom Tree

I'd like to be a pink blossom tree
And all the children will run to me,
Whilst they play and count to three.

But in the winter,
I'm as bald as a splinter,
I feel cold
And very old.

But in the spring I have power
And I begin to flower,
In the meadow,
As I begin to grow.

Sophie Johnson (11)
Christ Church CE Primary School

Wilf

My gran had a cat,
On her sofa he sat.

He'd got soft, dark fur and green eyes
Which couldn't tell any lies.

Wilf was that cat,
He dropped hair on the mat.

Wilf was so very old,
He even started going bald!

Wilf became a blurry blind,
We had to be ever so kind.

Kept banging his head,
Now he's dead.

Andrew Lee (10)
Dolphinholme CE Primary School

The Eagle, The Tiger And Me

I came across an eagle,
She was flying in the sky.
She looked so swift and brave, she was soaring way up high.

I came across an eagle,
She was happy, proud and free.
She could do amazing things and fly over the sea.

I came across an eagle,
She had so many skills.
She liked playing in the wind and racing over hills.

I came across an eagle,
I stroked her, she was soft.
She didn't like that very much - she bit my finger off!

Once I met a tiger,
He was very, very proud.
He was bold and brave and liked to roar out loud.

Once I met a tiger,
He was very, very big,
Padding around and not breaking a twig.

Once I met a tiger,
He was very, very hungry.
He stopped and licked his lips as soon as he saw me.

Once I met a tiger . . .
He ate me all up.
Now I'm in his tummy and I'm very, very stuck.

Natasha Ball (10)
Dolphinholme CE Primary School

A Day In The Garden

One day I was in the garden,
I saw a bumblebee,
It was sat among the flower beds,
I'm sure it winked at me.
The next day in the garden,
I saw a slimy snail,
Sunbathing on a cabbage leaf,
Getting nicely tanned without fail.
Again I was in the garden,
I saw a wriggly worm,
It was lying on the patio,
Having a cut and perm!
I found lots of bugs in the garden,
There were so many I could see,
I left them sitting there,
The snail, the worm and the bee.

Rebecca Hodgson (10)
Dolphinholme CE Primary School

My Horse And Me

I love my horse so very much,
But she always eats the cherry bush.

My mum shouts at her but it's of no use
And she only eats it when she gets let loose.

She's always thinking of her bucket of food,
If she doesn't get it she's in a bad mood.

If she carries on eating quite so much she'll get so very fat,
I try and hide her to get rid of it but I know I can't and that's that.

Jillian Hayhurst (10)
Dolphinholme CE Primary School

Monty

My dog is big,
My dog is bold,
My dog is never ever cold,
My dog will always wag his tail,
I never think he'll ever fail!

I love my dog very much,
He has never bitten anyone, yet,
He regularly takes a trip to the vet,
He only goes to check his weight,
He has one special mate!

Now this friend is Jarvis,
Who lives just next door,
When I've had an apple
He always eats the core,
He often goes and plays with him,
All day till the sky goes dim!

Jonathan Baines (10)
Dolphinholme CE Primary School

Rose's Nose

R ose loves to pick her nose,
O n the odd occasion she wipes it on her clothes,
S he always picks each nostril fairly,
E ven when it looks quite scary,
S he always manages to get her share in.

N aughty little nose provides her with all that gold,
O h it tastes so good, crunchy, creamy - just like blood.
S he never ever leaves it along,
E ven when she is in a deep, deep doze, as Rose just loves her nose.

Liam Withers (11)
Dolphinholme CE Primary School

I Saw My Teacher Shopping

I saw my teacher shopping
In ASDA she was there
Looking at the chocolate
I wondered if she would dare!

I always thought she was an alien
Do aliens eat chocolate too?
I watched from behind the cabbages
I'm sure her eyes flashed blue

She picked up the largest
Fruit and Nut bar
Then she firmly put it back on the shelf
Now I knew without a doubt because
No teacher would do that themself!

Class 5
Dolphinholme CE Primary School

My School

The teachers think they're features,
But they're only good preachers,
They preach all day about useless facts,
It's a real big issue,
When it comes to sport,
Football, rounders, skittleball, the lot!
I play them all, I love any game with a ball,
The girl that sits next to me thinks I'm a bit odd,
When I flick my rubber, I'm a real sod!
'James! Head's office now!' yelled my teacher,
Oh yes! I'm in a terrible mess!
Now I'll have to write another poem about the *head!*

James Bland (11)
Dolphinholme CE Primary School

Billy Bob

Billy is fluffy,
Billy is white.

Billy at night,
Goes out to hunt mice.

Billy is fat,
Billy is thin.

He only eats mice,
That bite him.

Billy's teeth are so small,
But his legs are very tall.

His eyes are blue
And he can see better than you.

Oliver Winder (11)
Dolphinholme CE Primary School

The Puzzles Of The Universe

The sun is a huge ball of fire,
The effect too close would be dire,
Though it travels across our sky each day,
Our teacher says it doesn't move in anyway!
The moon glistens in the night,
It is very, very bright,
In the darkness it looks so white,
But our teacher says it's not a source of light!
The stars twinkle their little lights,
Each and every one is a beautiful sight,
They form patterns though they make no sound,
But our teacher says at night they're found!
At last I believe my teacher knows best,
Now I'm ready for my SATs test.

Kirsty Mudd (11)
Dolphinholme CE Primary School

My Hamster

I've got a hamster,
Called Dandelion,
Bit of a nibbler,
But a friendly kind!
Always up to mischief,
Getting told off,
Likes the attention,
When she's not in a strop!
Little Miss Muffin,
Looks like that,
With her cheeks,
All full up!
She's going up to bed now,
Must be very tired,
Her bed is very cosy,
And I watch her being nosy!
She's got black pearls for eyes,
And a snowy-white body,
With one strip of grey,
Then add a little pink nose,
And that's my Dandelion!

Jacky King (10)
Dolphinholme CE Primary School

Sunset

S unset come tonight,
U ntil the morning light,
N ever go away,
S unset stay all day,
E ach and everyone,
T oday is sad now you have gone.

Jessica Wilson (10)
Dolphinholme CE Primary School

Who Likes . . . ?

Who likes crisps?
Me!
Who likes burgers?
Me!
Who likes chips?
Me!
Who likes yoghurt?
Me!
Who likes ketchup?
Me!
Who likes grapes?
Me!
Who likes bananas?
Me!
Who likes apples?
Me!
But best of all I like
Rice and curry, *slurp!*

Mohammed Oussama (10)
Hamer CP School

Countdown

'By the time I count to five
And you're still not doing your work
You're in trouble!
One . . . do your work!
Two . . .'
'I'm not doing it'
'Three . . . finish it or go to Mrs Smith
Four . . .'
'I'm not going to Mrs Smith'
'Five . . .'
'Oh no!'
'Come on, to Mrs Smith.'

Lewis Clark (10)
Hamer CP School

Who Likes . . . ?

Who likes speeding in cars?
Me!
Who likes racing motorbikes?
Me!
Who likes flying helicopters?
Me!
Who likes obstructing trucks?
Me!
Who likes riding bikes?
Me!
Who likes driving lorries?
Me!
But most of all I like
Flying in planes
Is there anything I don't like . . . ?
Yes . . .
You!

Tariq Mohammed (11)
Hamer CP School

Who Likes . . . ?

Who likes worms?
Me!
Who likes germs?
Me!
Who likes bugs?
Me!
Who likes frogs?
Me!
Who likes hogs?
Me!
Who likes big hairy spiders?
Me!
But best of all I like
Rats and fried onions!

Rose Tomlin (11)
Hamer CP School

Whisper, Whisper In The Village

Whisper, whisper
Whisper, whisper
Goes my sister
In the village

There are other
People who whisper
To each other
They carry on and on

I don't mind the
Whisper, whisper
Whisper, whisper
It's like a tune

Sometimes though
I wish the whisper
Would shut up soon.

Farah Imtiaz (11)
Hamer CP School

Who Likes . . . ?

Who likes apples?
Me!
Who likes chocolate?
Me!
Who likes veg?
Me!
Who likes gravy?
Me!
Who likes puddings?
Me!
But best of all I like
Veg, chicken, chips with lots
Of thick brown gravy.

Sophie Handley (11)
Hamer CP School

Who Likes . . . ?

Who likes fish?
Me!
Who likes chips?
Me!
Who likes custard?
Me!
Who likes chocolate?
Me!
Who likes apples?
Me!
Who likes beans?
Me!
Who likes peas?
Me!
Who likes jelly?
Me!
Who likes cheese?
Me!
Who likes yoghurt?
Me!
But best of all I like pizza and toast!

Saqib Ishaq (9)
Hamer CP School

Who Likes . . . ?

Who likes burgers?
Me!
Who likes chip butties?
Me!
Who likes cheese?
Me!
Who likes egg sandwiches?
Me!
But best of all I like
A chicken dinner, yum-yum!

Adam Dunnington (11)
Hamer CP School

Countdown

'If you don't come down by the time
I count to ten, you won't be going to your Grandma's house
One . . .'
'Where are my shoes?'
'Two . . .'
'They're in a knot'
'Three . . .'
'I can't find my socks'
'Four . . .'
'Now I need the toilet'
'Five, six . . .'
'Stop counting, please'
'Seven . . .'
'Where is my coat?'
'Eight . . .'
'Stop! Stop counting, please'
'Hurry up then'
'Nine . . .'
'Can I have some sweets?'
'No ten!'
'I am here! Grandma's, here we come!'

Nafisah Saleem (10)
Hamer CP School

I'll Have A . . .

I'll have a chip muppet please,
No! No!
I'll have a chip gravy,
Oh no, no! I mean
I'll have a sausage mole -
Sorry I mean an egg muttie,
Oh! I'll have a biscuit.

Saleha Begum (10)
Hamer CP School

Countdown

'If you don't come out of those bushes
By the time I count to ten
You're on the wall
One . . .'
'I'm not going on the wall'
'Two . . .'
'I don't know why you're counting
Because I'm not coming out'
'Three . . .
Stop giving back chat
Or else you're going to the head teacher
Four . . .'
'So what?'
'Five . . . !'
'Blah, blah, blah, blah'
'Six . . .
You might as well come out
Seven . . . !'
'Whatever!'
'Eight . . . !'
'Keep your hair on woman!'
'Nine . . . !'
'Go away, I'm not coming out!'
'Ten . . . !
Come on then to Mr Tonge!'

Chantelle Deloughrey (11)
Hamer CP School

Countdown

'If you are not in this line by the time
I count to ten, you will have a dinner time detention!
One . . .'
'No, I've only just come outside'
'Two . . .'
'Can you not see I'm coming?'
'Three . . .'
'C'mon, you're wastin' time'
'Shut up David, you muppet'
'Four . . .'
'I'm walking up - I can't go any faster'
'Five . . . I'm not having backchat off you!
I come to work to have a nice time not a horrible one
Six . . .'
(Muttering) 'Keep your hair on woman'
'Seven . . .'
'Whatever!'
'Eight . . . c'mon, now!
Nine . . .'
'I'm not having a dinner time detention!'
'Ten . . . *oh yes you are!*'

Aysha Ahmad (11)
Hamer CP School

Hate!

Hate is a red boiling lava
The taste of hate is
Like disgusting seawater
It smells like burnt sausages
It looks like the dark grey mist
Hate feels like a spiky hedgehog's back
That is *hate!*

Rowan Turnbull-Brown (9)
High Bentham CP School

Depression

The colour of depression is like a brown log floating behind a boat.
It tastes like a dirty stone stuck in your throat.
Smell of depression is like a mouldy shed,
Stuck in a forest of weeds and trees
And looks like a big cloud of black bees.
Depression sounds like people shouting and banging on bins.
Feeling depression is like rough, hard, scaly snake skin.
That is depression.

Elsa Priestley (10)
High Bentham CP School

Excitement

Excitement smells like the sweetest bunch of flowers.
It feels like the burning sun is in your hands
And looks like a garden on a summer's day.
The colour is bright pink with sky-blue spots.
Lots of singing birds in the air, that is the sound of excitement
And it tastes like sour-sweet all squashed up in your mouth.
That is excitement!

Shannon O'Hagan (10)
High Bentham CP School

Happiness

Happiness is the colour red and yellow - a sunset in the lake,
It feels like a soft silky cushion,
Happiness tastes like spaghetti - so succulent and juicy,
A warm fire, me snuggled up on the sofa,
The smell of happiness is a home-cooked meal, fresh from the oven,
That is *happiness!*

Beccy Lloyd (10)
High Bentham CP School

Sadness

When rain comes down fast and hard
It hits hard on the pavement, it is rain, rain, rain
Sadness is the colour of blue dying flowers
That taste of sadness is mould on bread
It smells like smoke filling the summer air
Sadness feels like something just hit you hard
It sounds like people laughing at you in the background
That is sadness!

Jack Harrison (10)
High Bentham CP School

Boredom

Boredom sounds like a shrill scream ringing in your ear.
It looks like a dull puddle of ink.
A smell of boredom lingers like the reek of a rotten egg.
Boredom feels like a hard stone grinding your teeth.
It tastes chewy and is hard to digest.
This is true boredom.

Ben Millings (9)
High Bentham CP School

Happiness

Happiness is red as some roses,
It smells like a yellow banana,
The taste of happiness is like ice cream,
Happiness is red like a love heart,
It feels like a sort of squashy cushion,
That is happiness.

David Adam (10)
High Bentham CP School

Hate

Hate is a red, dull apple, been left in a pot for ages,
It tastes of mouldy biscuits and lumpy potatoes,
The smell of hate is a pair of sweaty socks worn for two months,
Looks as mad as a wrestler's face which just lost a
championship battle
And it sounds like a lot of people shouting in the same room,
Hate feels as if you are getting kicked and hit lots of times.
That is hate.

Lauren O'Hagan (9)
High Bentham CP School

Happiness

Happiness is yellow like buttercups
It smells like red roses
The taste of happiness is like strawberries
Happiness is like shining stars
Happiness feels like soft teddies
That is happiness!

Andrew Procter (10)
High Bentham CP School

Fear!

Fear is a melting skull in a blazing ball of fire.
It smells like a fish jumping on your bed.
The taste is sour apple juice which has just been drunk.
The sound is a yelling wind echoing in the wind.
The colour is deep black like a thundering storm.
That is fear!

James Tuohy (10)
High Bentham CP School

Anger

Anger is as red as sour, mouldy tomatoes,
It smells like a smoky, burning fire.
The taste of anger is a sour red apple coming to poison you,
A red breath coming from an evil dragon,
That's the sight of anger
And it sounds like thunder rippling through the sky,
Stinging nettles ready to prick you,
That is what anger feels like,
That is anger!

Hattie Clay (9)
High Bentham CP School

Anger

It's like a howling wolf waiting for its dinner at midnight,
Anger is as red as a devil's fork,
A volcano waiting to erupt looks like anger,
The smell of a burning fire but you don't know where it is
And it feels like scolding lava burning your life away,
A horrible feeling,
That is anger.

Lewis Sharpe (10)
High Bentham CP School

Anger

Anger is stronger than thunder!
Anger smells like the hot steam of a steam train
The taste of anger is like burning coal
It's as mad as a fire and as red as a flame
Anger feels like the middle of a war
That's anger!

Isaac Dennis (9)
High Bentham CP School

Happiness

It is as bright as buttercups in a meadow swishing in the breeze
Happiness is as soft as a big fluffy dog
Sounds of children laughing and playing all day long
Meadows full of little lambs jumping like they are on springs
That's what happiness looks like
Smells of farms, haymaking in the evening breeze
Tastes of delicate chocolate melting in my mouth
That's what happiness is!

Stephanie Cowgill (10)
High Bentham CP School

Shock

Shock is as grey as rubble falling from a building
The sight of shock is a tidal wave heading right for you
And tastes like a cloud of dust entering your mouth
The feeling of shock is an earthquake with you in the centre
It sounds as if lightning has struck 1 foot from you
Smells like thin air from the Earth's atmosphere
That is shock!

David Lester (10)
High Bentham CP School

Happiness

Happiness is as bright as buttercup-yellow
Smells like freshly-made cream
The taste of happiness is like sweet butter
And it sounds like crispy leaves blowing in the breeze
Happiness feels soft as wool
It looks like a bunch of daffodils
That is happiness.

Faye Cook (10)
High Bentham CP School

Enjoyment

Enjoyment is a soft, silver, glowing chain,
It smells like the turkey at Christmas, cooking in the oven,
The enjoyment tastes like the juice of an ice cream dripping
                                             into your mouth,
You felt like you're swimming in the light blue sea with the
                                water gushing up your body,
Enjoyment looks like a gold diamond watch glowing,
Sounds of the ducks quacking while you're on a river walk.

Jordan Armstrong (9)
High Bentham CP School

Hate

Hate feels prickly and sharp like a lime-green thorn,
It looks like a bomb ticking, ready to explode,
The taste of hate is like sour milk trickling down your throat,
Black as a back alley with no streetlight
And the sound of hate is people shouting loud, snarly comments
And the smell of hate is a ghastly smoke from a burning house.
That's hate!

Sara Carter (10)
High Bentham CP School

Pain

Pain is blue like the sky
And smells like sick,
It tastes like the salty sea,
Pain is a stormy night and someone hitting you
And looks like a damp, grotty house in the city,
It feels like a thorn stabbing into you.
That is pain!

Connor Hall (9)
High Bentham CP School

Happiness

Happiness is bright yellow corn swaying in a field,
It smells like freshly-made popcorn,
The taste of happiness tastes like chocolate sweets bought
                                        from the shop.
Happiness, it feels like you are sleeping in a bed of feathers
And it sounds like a bird singing all day long.
Yellow flowers standing up straight, that's what happiness looks like.
That is happiness.

Hayley Mace (9)
High Bentham CP School

Sadness

Sadness is as grey as water clouds full of rain.
It sounds like silence in the countryside.
The sight of a raven flying lonely in the air,
The taste of a sour lemon is sadness.
Feels like a heavy heart,
Smells like a musty attic.

Liam Ellershaw (10)
High Bentham CP School

My Life

My mum, Teresa is the best,
My dad, John is better than the rest,
My brother, Stuart is always dirty,
My brother, Andrew is rather flirty,
My cat, Josh is adopted by my best friend
Nicolle Jayne Burlison.

Alison Clark (10)
Mayfield Primary School

My Little Sister

When my sister went to the toilet
I flushed her down the drain
She swirled right down to the bottom
And I never saw her again
Three weeks later I heard her moan
'You've broke the chain and my backbone'
She pinched my back so I flushed her back
And then I didn't see her again
At teatime she came up to the surface
And shouted, 'Where's mine?'
So Dad ran upstairs and said, 'Danielle, don't whine'
Within five minutes Daddy said, 'Please Danielle
Will you go to sleep instead?'

Charlotte Salt (11)
Mayfield Primary School

Swimming

Heart beats faster,
Lungs pant,
Feel the water rush against your face,
Faster and faster you swim,
You're gasping for air,
You're nearly at the finish line,
One more pace to go,
You're ahead of the rest,
You pass the finish line,
The crowd cheers louder and louder,
Your heart aches,
You're gasping for air and breath,
You won the race, hooray!

Rebecca Hulley (11)
Mayfield Primary School

If My Grandad Was Here Right Now
(For my grandad, Tony)

If my grandad was here right now
He'd probably be building a wall,
Maybe a garage or an extension,
Whichever large or small.

If my grandad was here right now,
He'd probably not have his teeth in,
But both of his hardworking hands
Would be in the yummy sweet tin!

If my grandad was here right now,
He'd probably be telling humorous jokes
Or placing a bet on horses,
With the other blokes.

If my grandad was here right now,
He'd probably be loving his family,
Especially my grandma,
But at least now he's not in pain and he is set free!

Sophie Lees (11)
Mayfield Primary School

Life

Life is a present, a gift to all,
It's like a block of gold to things great and small,
Life is precious, amazing and fun,
Although we have rain, we do get sun,
Life is happiness now and is all around,
Life can be silent or full of sound,
Life is funny and completely cool,
Life is splashing in a swimming pool,
Life has got to end, boo-hoo,
Life is me and life is you.

Samantha Irving (10)
Mayfield Primary School

My Family Is So Weird

My family is so weird
My mum has grown a bear
My brother is a pussy cat
And he won't let go of my bat
My dad looks like my mother
My cat looks like my brother
I am the only ordinary one
My sister looks like my pet swan
All my family's upside-down
Because my grandma is a clown
Now my family's back together
It is the end of my rhyme
Now it is all over
It is my bedtime.

Patrick Tobin (11)
Mayfield Primary School

My Family

My house is like a zoo
With a sister that reminds me of a lion
Who makes a lot of noise
My mum is like a big, cuddly bear
Who is always very loving and caring
My dad is like a tortoise
Because he is always in his garage and we never see him
And me, well, I am just like a rabbit
That always likes to rest . . .
But sometimes I'm like the Tasmanian Devil
When I am running around and being clumsy
And that's why my family call me Taz!

Nicolle Burlison (11)
Mayfield Primary School

Football Crazy

Toes in
Bellies in
Legs in
Get your ball
You've practised in the hall
Give 'em a bow
Off you go
Get a goal
Penalty shot
In the net
Get back
Do it again
3, 2, 1
Whistle goes
Two mins extra time
Get another, you can do it
Whistle goes
Shake hands
What a good game
Do that again next time
And I'll buy you a butty for
Dinnertime.

Kelsey Swales (10)
Mayfield Primary School

All Of My Dreams

All of my dreams are in my head
Most of them are in bed
They're normally bad
And make me sad
I cuddle my ted
I dread the next time I get in bed
I wake up shivering with my mum next to me
And that is the end of the bad night in bed.

Rachel Eaton (11)
Mayfield Primary School

The Everyday Alphabet

A is for Ashley who is utterly mad,
B is for Busted, my favourite band,
C is for Chloe, my best friend,
D is for Dommy, my favourite sister,
E is for a rotten egg, smelly or what?
F is for fire, quick run, get out of here!
G is for girls that fancy boys,
H is for Henry that smells bad,
 I is for India, the country,
J is for Jason who is always naughty,
K is for Katie who is kind,
L is for Lee, my brother-in-law,
M is for Mayfield School, that's my school,
N is for Nathan who is a good runner,
O is for orange, very sour,
P is for Polly, my little dog,
Q is for Queenie, my friend's dog,
R is for Rebecca who is my other best friend,
S is for Sarah, my mum's name,
T is for Twiggy who is as tall as a tree,
U is for umbrellas that keep you dry in the rain,
V is for vase for pretty flowers,
W is for water fights that happen in the summer,
X is for X-ray, I've never had one,
Y is for Yasmin who is a tomboy,
Z is for Zoe, my friend.

Rosie Sutton (10)
Mayfield Primary School

Hands

Hands can clap, slap and tap
Hands help you make, bake and shake
Hands steal, peel and feel
Hands can turn, hands can burn
Hands can write a poem.

Mark Holme (10)
Mayfield Primary School

Best Friends

B est friends from the start,
E ach brain
S tarted mind-reading,
T hey were getting freaked out.

F orever they will be
R eading each other's minds forever,
I f they are normal they do not know,
E ven though they will still be friends,
N ow they are still wondering why,
D o they know each other too well?
S omeone might have cast a spell.

D ouble act they are,
O h when will they know?
U nderstanding each other's words, will they
B e friends for long?
L iving a double life, is it
E asy?

A best friend like you, how
C ooooool!
T wins from the day they were born.

Katie Cartwright (11)
Mayfield Primary School

Mayfield

M ayfield school is the best
A star has just come in and that's me
Y ou should come to this school
F un you will have, it's great
I have been here all my life, so you should too
E njoy this school
L ovely Mayfield, come here
D islike the bullying because we have none.

Matthew Goddard (11)
Mayfield Primary School

Hands

Your hands can clap,
Your hands can slap,
Your hands can take,
Your hands can make,
Your hands can drink,
Your hands can link,
Your hands can wipe,
Your hands can swipe,
Your hands can heal,
Your hands can steal,
Your hands can hold,
Your hands can mould,
Your hands can write,
Your hands can fight,
Your hands can fix,
Your hands can mix.

Jack Herring (10)
Mayfield Primary School

Hands

Hands can feel, steal and heal
Hands can slap, tap and clap
Hands can pinch, hands can clinch
Hands can punch or help you eat lunch
Hands can hit, hands can dig a pit
Hands can stack, hands can smack
Hands can run the tap, hands can read a map
Hands can poke, hands can smoke
Hands can choke, hands can stroke
Hands can beat a bloke.

Connor Grady (10)
Mayfield Primary School

Fireworks!

F lying high,
I n the sky,
R aining sparks
E verywhere,
W ill they bang or will they pop?
O ver and over again they fly,
R ight and left they zoom by
K ids are amazed by the flashing bright colours,
S hining lights in the sky!

Laura Williams (11)
Mayfield Primary School

Hands

Hands are helpful at school
They help to draw
Hands help the judge
To hammer down the law
Hands help to pick and throw
And help to bake a cake
Hands help to stroke a cat
They are for a hand to shake.

Rachel Gartside (10)
Mayfield Primary School

Colours Of Day

Green is like the blades of grass swaying
Red is like the sky turning dark
Purple is like an explosion in the woods
Yellow is like the sun shining in the sky
Blue is the sky way up above us
White is the clouds floating above.

Callum Entwistle (10)
Mayfield Primary School

Capture

I want to capture the sound of laughter
Of my sister when I come home from school,
I want to capture the silence of the cold winter months,
I want to capture the smell of the sea and keep it forever,
I want to capture the taste of fresh, red strawberries,
I want to capture the feel of the wind blowing in my face,
I want to capture the moment when my sister and cousin
First came into my life,
I want to capture the sight of my cat's proud face
And hold onto it like a picture,
I want to capture the feeling of a warm, loving hug from my nan,
I want to capture the memory of the last biscuit I gave to Scooby.

Rebecca Bellingham (10)
Mayfield Primary School

Catching Time!

I want to capture the sound of wind whistling in the frosty winter,
I want to capture the sight of my great grandad's wrinkly
                                        hand holding mine,
I want to capture the lingering smell of an empty sweet barrel,
I want to capture the feel of my dog's wet nose pressing to mine,
I want to capture the feeling of hatred and drown it in a river
                                        of happy tears,
I want to capture the taste of my grandma's homemade apple pie,
I want to capture the memory of my little sister's first words,
I want to capture the moment when I saw all my family
                                        in one room, happy!

Sarah Davies (10)
Mayfield Primary School

Things I Want To Keep

I want to capture the sound of my mum and dad saying I love you
I want to capture the feel of my family kissing me
I want to capture the smell of my nana and grandad's house
I want to capture the sight of the birds flying high in the sky
I want to capture the taste of my mum's lovely roast cooking
                                                    in the oven
I want to capture the moment when I was born and found that
                              I had the best family in the world
I want to capture the memory of when my grandad was ill and
                                                  he didn't die
I want to capture the silence of my sister and brother snoring
I want to capture the feeling of my nan cuddling me.

Leoni Grenfell (10)
Mayfield Primary School

I Want To Capture . . .

I want to capture the sound of my kitten's miaowing,
I want to capture the feel of a snake when I first felt one,
I want to capture the smell of my very first Christmas dinner,
I want to capture the first sight of my dog,
I want to capture the taste of chicken in the oven,
I want to capture the moment of playing with my friends,
I want to capture the memory of my grandad Bill and nanna Joyce,
I want to capture the silence of the swimming pool when
                                        nobody is in it,
I want to capture the feeling of joy and peace.

Hayley Coombes (10)
Mayfield Primary School

Hands

Hands throw, hands row,
Hands draw, hands saw,
Hands steal, hands peel
Very raw potatoes.

Hands rub, hands scrub,
Hands wriggle, hands jiggle,
Hands twist, hands insist
On what you want to do.

Hands write, hands fight,
Hands dig, hands jig,
Hands hit, hands sit
On your blue school chair!

Lexi Ogden (10)
Mayfield Primary School

Hands

Hands rub, hands scrub
Hands hit, hands knit
Hands scratch and scrape
Hands are a funny shape
They wiggle in water and jiggle in sand
I love my hands, they do so much
They pull and push and grab and touch
They hold and mould and twist and turn
Until I am in a concern
My hands, they do a lot for me
They pour me a cup of tea.

Katie Rourke (10)
Mayfield Primary School

Hands

Hands lift and drop.
Hands splash and swim.
Hands scratch and punch.
Hands wiggle and squiggle.
Hands push and pull.
Hands poke and pinch.
Hands pick and touch.
Hands are great.
Hands colour and paint.
Hands tap and clap.
Hands steer and shake.
Hands are fun.

Heather Brooks (10)
Mayfield Primary School

Hands

Hands can slap and clap
Hands can do press-ups
Hands slash, hands carry cash
Or serve out the mash,
Hands can do anything,
They can wave, tap, turn, catch,
Fix, paint, pull, push, throw,
What are hands for?
Stack, rip, pick up?
What are hands for?
Hug, offer friendship
And hands can give you love.

Shelby Newton (9)
Mayfield Primary School

Hands

Hands can eat meat or drink fresh water,
Hands can pull or push doors,
Hands can turn the lights on or they can turn the lights off,
Hands can throw in your fishing rod then wind the rod back in,
Hands can break things then mend them,
Hands can help you by holding your book and they can put
it down again,
Hands can protect people's faces or fight back,
Hands can play or they can rest,
Hands can type or they can write.

Liam McCallion (10)
Mayfield Primary School

Lobden Golf Course

L is for long shot
O is for out of bounds
B is for big course
D is for driver
E is for eighth hole
N is for nine over par

G is for greened it
O is for off the tee
L is for landing in the plantation
F is for fair play

C is for clubhouse
O is for good shot out
U is for under par
R is for in the rough
S is for sandy bunker
E is for enjoy it on Lobden Golf Course.

Jack Broxup (10)
Our Lady & St Anselm's RC Primary School

My Dream

My dream is to play rugby
For England's national team,
I have been playing since I was 8,
Now that is my *biggest dream!*

The flagpole's waving in the wind
And when you get tackled,
You are definitely *pinned!*

The ball slipping from hand to hand
And when you're in a ruck you'll hit the *land!*

And at the end of the match it is good to know
You have won, so very so!

Nathan Fowles (11)
Our Lady & St Anselm's RC Primary School

Dancing For The Rest Of My Life!

When I'm past my high school years
And when I'm starting to drink beers,
I want to become a pro dancer
And help a charity to raise money, such as cancer.

When I get old, lonely and have grey hair,
I won't really care,
Because I'll be dancing around my home,
My kids will get embarrassed and begin to moan,
(But I won't care).

Dancing is my life and will stay that way,
No one can change that, okay!

Bethany O'Malley (10)
Our Lady & St Anselm's RC Primary School

Favourite Things!

Crisps and chocolate,
Yummy, yummy,
All these things,
Fill up my tummy.

Meeting other children,
This is also great,
On holidays and in parks,
I just love to communicate.

Sometimes I listen,
To music in my head,
'Get up right now, you lazy thing,'
My mother always said.

I also love to talk,
I talk all night and day,
I never stop to take a breath,
'I'll die one day,' I say.

I sometimes like to write,
Horrors and fun stories,
All the things I have written about
Are my hobbies and my glories.

Hannah Robinson (10)
Our Lady & St Anselm's RC Primary School

My Teacher

My teacher is very nice,
But sometimes is as hot as spice,
She tells lots of funny jokes to you
And maybe makes your dreams come true!

Once you see her, you'll think she's great!
She may feel that you're her best mate,
So sit down and have a cup of tea,
She's as nice as ever can be!

Lois Vail (10)
Our Lady & St Anselm's RC Primary School

My Hamster

I have a hamster
Which is energetic and funny

But there's a problem
He doesn't come out when it's sunny

He is a cute hamster
I remember when I first got him

He is a white and brown hamster
When I got him, he was really slim

My hamster was bought
Now he is a bit chubby

But the best thing of all . . .
He's my cuddly hamster.

Kieran Ryan (11)
Our Lady & St Anselm's RC Primary School

My Dream

Footie is my hobby,
Like the England legend Bobby,
Hopwood City, Stockport,
Footie is my hobby.

Footie is my dream,
I'm in a ladies team,
Kick it, shoot it, head it, boot it,
Footie is my dream.

I'm football mad,
I take after my dad,
All I think about is footie, footie, footie,
I'm just football mad!

Alex Foster (10)
Our Lady & St Anselm's RC Primary School

School!

I love school, it's the best,
It's even better than my vest,
You might think I'm a fool,
But I still love school.

I love school, it's my life,
It's even better than my knife,
There is a rule,
But I still love school.

I love school, it's very good,
It's even better than some mud,
You might think it's cruel,
But I love school.

Jessica Claxton (10)
Our Lady & St Anselm's RC Primary School

My Dad

My dad is the best,
Better than all the rest.
He doesn't bother, he doesn't care,
But he loves me anywhere.

He may be small and not that tall,
He is quite strong,
But he can't sing a song.

I love my dad,
But he can get mad,
But then he makes me very sad.

He's called Geoff,
Why, I don't know,
But I do know he's the best father I've ever known.

Megan Hall (10)
Our Lady & St Anselm's RC Primary School

Best Mum

Favourite things, favourite things,
Not my mother when she sings.

I love my mother,
More than any other.

Favourite things, favourite things,
My mother is better than queens and kings.

I love my mother,
More than any other.

Favourite things, favourite things,
More colourful than a butterfly's beautiful wings.

My mother!

Michaela McDonald (10)
Our Lady & St Anselm's RC Primary School

Dreamland

Dreamland is my land,
Where all my dreams come true,
I only dream of what to do,
Everything I'm saying is very true,
This is what I would do.

Eat chocolate all day,
Then jump to May,
I like to have a friend,
But my friendship came to an end.

Liam Blackmore (10)
Our Lady & St Anselm's RC Primary School

My Hamster, Nibbles

N is for nibble star,
I is for insulator,
B is for brilliant,
B is for brave,
L is for liberty,
E is for especially,
S is for a super pet.

I is for invincible,
S is for saint.

T is for tame,
H is for hero,
E is for excellent.

B is for the best,
E is for energetic,
S is for soft,
T is for terrific!

Rory Troughton (10)
Our Lady & St Anselm's RC Primary School

Fashion

Do you know my passion?
My passion is for fashion.
I love to shop every Saturday,
Even though I have to pay!
I roam around, I don't care,
I go to McDonald's, I meet my friends there,
I drive my mates round the bend,
Cos I'm the one who sets the trend.
Well, really I just love to shop
And trust me, I will never stop!

Amber Whitehead (10)
Our Lady & St Anselm's RC Primary School

My Favourite Cars

I like to travel far and far
In my bright red Ferrari car

I like to drive fast and slow
In my Fiesta, that is yellow

I love driving down the motorway
In my Jaguar, the colour grey

I like driving very, very fast
If I go round that bend any faster it will be my last

I like motorbikes, Ferraris and Jaguars
And I also like Fiestas and TVRs.

Harry Peters (10)
Our Lady & St Anselm's RC Primary School

My Dad

My dad is the best,
Better than all the rest.
He doesn't bother to wear a vest,
At least he hasn't been told he's under arrest.

My dad was stupid,
But then he got hit by Cupid,
He fell in love with my mum
And she said he had a big bum.

My dad is the best
Even though he is a
Pest!

Jessica Wilkinson (10)
Our Lady & St Anselm's RC Primary School

An Icy Pond

The shimmering pond was frozen
It was glowing in the light

There once was a frozen pond
That shimmered and glimmered
And glimmered and shimmered
There once was a frozen pond

The pond was small and like a ball
That very small shimmering pond

It was overgrown but had lots of fish
That very small shimmering pond

The fish it had were red and white
They ate small shrimps
And sometimes mites
Those fish the small pond had

It had frogs that fight
Insects that bite
And lots of other life

It smells like hogs
But has lots of frogs
That very old, small, frozen pond.

Michael Yaxley (9)
Ribby With Wrea Endowed CE Primary School

My Family

My family are the best,
They're better than the rest.
My mum is kind,
She helps me to find,
Bobbles and bangles of every kind.

My dad gets stressed
And sometimes thinks me a pest.
My cousins are so cool,
But not Vincent, he's a fool.

My nan gets me sweets,
Otherwise little treats.
My grandad is very friendly,
Also very trendy.

My grandma helps me at home,
On things I can't do alone.
My grandad Barrie is the best,
In the afternoon he always has a rest.

My family does funny things,
When music comes on my grandma sings,
My family have done things I wished they hadn't done,
But I still love them just the way they come.

Sophie Jones (10)
Ribby With Wrea Endowed CE Primary School

My Family

My sister is gentle and kind,
My nanna's incredible,
My auntie, I can't believe she's my auntie,
My uncle's in the pot of spice,
One day so beautiful,
One day so hot and
One day so sugared with love,
I love them all, all tonight and
They love me too tonight,
My mum is so gorgeous,
I love her so much,
She's like a cloud in the sky,
My grandad is so funny,
My cousin is so handsome,
My other cousin is a rock star in the sky,
I love them all so much,
They spoil me too much.

Danielle Keady (9)
Ribby With Wrea Endowed CE Primary School

Going On Our Trip

Go to the toilet and get your packed lunch
'Ow! Miss, Ben just give me a punch'
'It's time to go'
'No, I'm sitting with Joe'
'Does it matter? Just stop being a dunce'

'Oh Miss, are we there yet?'
'No, we've just set off, Collette'
'I know, let's sing a song'
'Don't you sing, you're like King Kong'
'Whoa reverse, there's a water jet'

'Turn around, you've missed it'
'Everyone off, come back in a bit'
'It's a shame Dan's hurt his leg, he'll have to hop'
'Awesome! Hey wanna race to the gift shop?'

Thomas Leach (10)
Ribby With Wrea Endowed CE Primary School

My Family

My family is kind and cheerful
They are fun and have games
They dance around, prance around
Not my family today
People singing, people swinging
Dancing around today
My brother is funny, makes me laugh
Picks me up, puts me down
Spins me around, he walks away
My friends make me laugh
They are kind
And when I'm sad
They cheer me up
My cousins are fun and friendly
They join in with games
They laugh and sing
They dance and prance
That's my cousins today.

Alexandra Hodson (11)
Ribby With Wrea Endowed CE Primary School

A Winter Countryside

Sparkling icicles hanging from the grass,
Ducks go skating along the shimmering glass,
Horses wrapped up in their snugly coats,
Chomping away on mouth-watering oats,
Hills up high with crisp white hats,
Searching for scraps of food are rats,
A little house sits far away,
A farmer is out getting bales of hay,
Inside a fire is burning, warming his toes,
When will twinkling stars come out?
Nobody knows.

Laura Fenton (10)
Ribby With Wrea Endowed CE Primary School

My Family

First of all I'll start with my dad
Not very often does he make me sad
My dad is so cool
He also likes to play pool

Next in the line is my brother, Max
He likes to play with his plastic axe
My brother is very funny, but silly
He really loves chilli

Last, but not least, is my mum
When listening to music she likes to hum
My mum sometimes is annoying (not)
When tying she likes to use complicated knots

So that is my family, nice but crazy
Just like me.

Jack Warrington (11)
Ribby With Wrea Endowed CE Primary School

New Life

In the soil below,
Seeds are growing, bulging, popping,
Roots will sprout, then the shoot,
The leaves are growing, new life is here,
Producing slowly through the day.

In the fields animals are born,
They play about in the grass,
The cows are mooing, the lambs are baaing,
The sign of new life is here,
Producing slowly through the day.

In the night the fox cubs play,
Playing till the bright new morning comes,
The badgers play just like the cubs,
The sign of new life is here,
Producing slowly through the day.

Thomas Yaxley (11)
Ribby With Wrea Endowed CE Primary School

Going On Our School Trip

Going on our trip today
Happy and jolly all the way
People shouting
People mounting
Not on our trip today

Josh making
People baking
Not on our trip today
People dancing
While people prancing
Not on our trip today

On our trip we visit hats
Hats with bats
Hats with cats
That's our trip today.

Daniel Hinde (11)
Ribby With Wrea Endowed CE Primary School

Rural Wrea Green

R iver running by the road
U nder the rock lives a toad
R abbits run about in the fields
A ll the birds lay their eggs in their nest
L apwing fly off to the west

W here the cows graze the lush green grass
R elaxing farmers watch the cows in the fields
E ndless field of animals slowly disappear
A gricultural fields start to grow a dark green colour

G reen fields all around
R ows and rows of bright green fields
E vening comes and all the animals find somewhere to rest
E very farmer has got the work off their chest
N othing stirs in the dark of the night.

Peter Pilkington (11)
Ribby With Wrea Endowed CE Primary School

The Winter House

A cold, frosty winter scene
In the middle of a dark mysterious forest
Icy slate grey roof tiles
Cover the lonely, rundown dwelling
Frozen, stone-cold icicles
Hang down from the grotty channel

The mossy, dirty tree is bare
The red, green or golden leaves
Have clear artic ice trapping them
The frizzy fruit bush
With berries as red as a demon's eyes
Drips chilly, freezing water off the white snow

The wind is cruising through the garden
Like a roaming ferry in the ocean
The grass is laden down with dew
Which drips all through the tiring 24 hours
The grass is dying from the ice
The worm in the soil doesn't find it very nice

The house is old and weary
But the delightful scene is young
A carpet of white covers the grass
And a carpet of grey clouds cover the sky
The winter house is getting old
And finally it's deserted to rest in peace.

Joe Walsh (10)
Ribby With Wrea Endowed CE Primary School

A New Life

As springtime arrives new life is born,
The morning dew on the wet, damp lawn,
The sun is scorching bright and high,
I dance and sing as the birds fly by.

The flowers sway in the morning breeze,
We hear the buzz of the passing bees,
The butterfly flies up high in the air,
Do you see the galloping George's mare?

The pond is glistening, shiny, full
Of fish that feed the hungry gull,
So as the day soon drives to an end,
I know that I have got a friend.

As I sit staring up at the candyfloss clouds,
The lonely will leans as it bows,
The birds grow silent,
The sky becomes dark
And all you can hear is the singing lark.

Another day is yet to begin,
My room is slowly growing dim,
But now my dreams dance in my mind,
I dream of new life and springtime rhymes!

Hailey Voyle (11)
Ribby With Wrea Endowed CE Primary School

Winter's Love

As the autumn dies away,
Winter's love comes out to play,
The land frosts over,
From Scotland to Dover,
As winter's love is born.

A sheet of ice covers the ponds
And the church bells begin to dong,
The leaves turn crispy
And the moors become misty,
As winter's love is born.

It soon turns March
And the frost on the bamboo arch,
Shimmers as it melts away,
From winter to spring,
New life begins
And winter's love is forlorn.

Kieran McSpirit (11)
Ribby With Wrea Endowed CE Primary School

Untitled

Summer has come, spring has broken
Tulips from their bulb have awoken
The lamb has grown from its old form
The sun is out keeping the earth so warm

Autumn has come, summer came to die
My mum is making delicious apple pie
The leaves are falling from the trees
Drifting slowly, gently in the breeze

Winter has come, autumn has passed
Now is not the time to drink an ice blast
Now the pond shimmers in the moonlight
Giving off a brilliant light that is some sight

Spring has come, autumn has gone
Me and my brother are throwing sand bombs
The sun has come out, the chill of winter gone
I saw a bunch of ducklings and I named one Don.

Patrick Parr (10)
Ribby With Wrea Endowed CE Primary School

Winter Village

Snowflakes falling from the sky,
Snow drifts down from Heaven,
Loads of tinsel and baubles to buy,
How many weeks to Christmas? Seven!

Nests are deserted, birds are gone,
Not a blackbird or thrush's song,
Peace is running through the air,
Silence, silence everywhere.

Crisp white snow is on the floor,
Tinsel hangs upon the doors,
Icicles hang from frozen trees,
There is even ice on their leaves.

Snowmen settle on children's lawns,
They start to melt as summer dawns,
Winter came, came to die,
The sun is blazing in the sky.

Ben Jones-Dale (10)
Ribby With Wrea Endowed CE Primary School

In The Meadows

Through a meadow full of lush green grass
A river flows whilst the seasons pass
The lambs frolic in the spring sunshine
Their coat is so woolly and looks so fine
The birds fly out in the morning breeze
The perfect weather for all the bees

The wind blows gently through the trees
The breeze blows pollen which can make people sneeze
The birds flutter silently through the air
Their astonishing formations can make people stare
The birds pad softly across the ground
Their wonderful voice is a beautiful sound

In the rich green field gallop several horses
They and the cows aren't enemy forces
Beside the meadow is a narrow dirt track
The horses often stop for a short grass snack
The cows graze in the bright green grassland
The grass is lush down to every strand.

Helen Cropper (10)
Ribby With Wrea Endowed CE Primary School

My Family

First of all I'll start with my mum,
She cooks me food and fills my tum.
She has a horse called Stert,
Who's always covered in dirt.
She thought of my nickname, Bash,
(And also thought of the trash!)

Now I'll talk about my dad,
Who never in his life has been sad.
All he does is work in the night,
But in the day he's always bright.
He's got a smile that lights up my life,
He is a sharp thinker, just like a knife.

Next we'll talk about my bro,
Who's doing a rap in the talent show.
He listens to music, night and day,
To clean the house, they have to pay.
He gets £15 every week,
Before he shouts, he needs to speak.

My sister's name is Samantha,
She prances around, just like a panther.
She's gone to Ibiza for half a year,
On the phone she talks, we hear.
She now has a fiancé called Adam,
Who likes to call her a madam.

My stepdad is called Tony,
Who was the one who got my pony.
He is the manager of our farm
And treats my mum like a ma'am.
Most of the time he cooks the tea
And is a great stepdad, just to me.

Ashley Harding (11)
Ribby With Wrea Endowed CE Primary School

School Trip

Everybody's excited for the day ahead,
But I'm still tired, want to go to bed.
Hate the journey there,
Love the actual stay,
Don't want to leave,
Never get my way.
Fossils, stones and animals too,
What to come join in?
Fun for me and you.
Lunch's yummy,
In my tummy,
Sandwich and jam,
Bread and ham,
Still have some fun,
Maybe in the sun,
Come on, we better go,
'No,' we say, 'no!'

Rachel Cara (10)
Ribby With Wrea Endowed CE Primary School

Matilda

Matilda's parents hated her
They even had an affair

Matilda enjoyed reading books
And even though she had good looks

Matilda's mum went to bingo
She read a book about a dingo

Matilda went to a school on her street
Her teacher, Miss Honey, was very sweet

Miss Trunchbull chucked her in the slammer
Then she chucked a very big hammer

Matilda visited Miss Honey's cottage
For a sandwich of sausage.

William Hargreaves (11)
St James' CE Primary School, Chorley

The Fight For Love

A man came riding
Into the old cottage inn
His name was James
And he went over to the bin

He met a girl called Tiffany
Grabbed her and gave her a kiss
A boy called Sam saw him
While the night was very dim

Sam got a gun
He knew he would come
James came again
Sam shot him while eating a bun

Tiffany finally married
Jacob, she thought he was cute
They bought a dog
And named it Beaut.

Sam Tait (10)
St James' CE Primary School, Chorley

Matilda

Matilda was a young girl
Who was always like a little pearl
She was a little liar
Who deserved to be on fire

Matilda sat in her very big home
And began to groan
A spark lit up
She ran downstairs for a cup

She rang the fire brigade
And drunk some lemonade
She read a book
With good looks!

John Worthington (9)
St James' CE Primary School, Chorley

The Beast

As night crept over the town like an infinite sheet of black satin
The moon was a diamond hanging in the sky
Hiding its face from the evil that was about to descend
Upon a small town,
As the knight entered the village he was met by a hunch-backed
Stranger, 'You . . .' the knight muttered as he drew his sword
And faced the stranger, who let out a horrid shriek and lunged
At the knight, 'Ha . . . you fool' laughed the knight
As he finished the stranger

He travelled to the dark mountains, 'He is close . . .'
And as though he had appeared from thin air
A second stranger jumped at him
But before he could draw his sword the creature grabbed him
And whispered, 'If I'm going, you're coming with me'
At that they both plunged into the abyss
They say that on misty nights you can hear the knight
And the stranger battling.

Philip Robert Smalley-Morris (11)
St James' CE Primary School, Chorley

Flimpto

Flimpto the fire-breathing dragon
Spikes on his back and a point on his tail
Mrs Sippy was walking down the street when
She was crushed to the floor.
The young girl
Melony, had a troubled day with her dogs
Flimpto, the fire-breathing dragon was off to the rescue
The dogs were home, back to the bedroom for
Flimpto, the fire-breathing dragon.

Andrew McAllister (10)
St James' CE Primary School, Chorley

Matilda

Aunt Elizabeth sat in the lovely garden,
Thinking about little Matilda,
She wondered why she began to die
And I wondered what had hurt her.

Aunt Elizabeth was very mad,
Steam was coming from her head,
Matilda went to bed,
Without being fed.

Matilda called the firemen of England,
In a second they were here,
The lights were flashing,
The firemen were dashing.

The firemen went,
Not any sign of fire,
The crowd said lair,
The firemen were tired.

A spark was lit in the house,
Matilda was doomed
And she had a wound,
She waved and said, 'Fire!'

When Aunt Elizabeth got back,
No Matilda, no house!

Liam Sharrock (9)
St James' CE Primary School, Chorley

Matilda

Aunt Elizabeth sat in the garden
And she went off and said goodbye,
Eating lemon pie, she thought
About Matilda and made her cry.

Doris came knocking on the door,
She had a baby, rocking,
Doris came bending down on the floor,
Is Tim alright? Has he died?
No, he has not.

He's fine, he's on holiday with Aunt Phyllis,
'Well,' Matilda said, 'he died.'
'Matilda, not again,' she sent her to bed.

Aunt Elizabeth went to the theatre
And when she came back, no house
And no Matilda.

Cara Wishart (8)
St James' CE Primary School, Chorley

Matilda

Matilda is so good like a cat on a wall,
Matilda and her mum went to the school hall,
Her mum, Sally, heard the bell ring,
It was her dad, he came in a ping.

Matilda and her dad went to the zoo,
They found an old shoe,
Mum lost her hat,
Matilda's dad bought a rat.

Mum and Dad came with me to the hall,
She killed the cat, no more of that.

Sarah Jepson (9)
St James' CE Primary School, Chorley

Alice And The Alien

Alice went to the park with a shark
And the shark gave a loud bark,
'Be quiet you crazy dog,
You're as noisy as a warthog.'

Suddenly she saw something in the air,
It was a complete nightmare,
Then it landed on some grass,
Where there was some trash.

It was a tiny rocket,
Could it fit in my pocket?
The top was like a shiny pan,
Then out popped a little man.

A shy little girl said, 'Go away
And come back another day.'
Lots of people tried to chase him off,
Then Alice shouted, 'Stop.'

She soon sent him back to his nation,
So they all had a celebration,
Crunchy crisps, fizzy pop, fairy cakes.

Georgia Richardson (8)
St James' CE Primary School, Chorley

Matilda

Aunt Elizabeth
Sat in the garden
Thinking about Matilda
She began to cry
Why did she have to die?
She was such a liar
Always pretending there was fire
Matilda was such a liar
But stand by her.

Daniel McDonald (10)
St James' CE Primary School, Chorley

Harry Potter's Big Mistake

Harry woke up at twelve o'clock
He heard a knock, knock, knock
Ron and Hermione were in shock
The clock went tick tock

It was already past noon
When Harry could see the moon
He remembered when Hagrid called Dad a prune

They had missed the train
What a shame
They heard people call a name

They flew in an amazing car
They didn't get very far
The car crashed into some sticky tar
And that is the end so far.

Sophie Davies (9)
St James' CE Primary School, Chorley

The Zoo

In the zoo there is a lion
Has an owner whose name is Ryan.
There is a panda
Whose name is Miranda.

In the zoo there is a snake
Who likes to eat a piece of cake.
There also is a crocodile
Who leaves his waste in a very big pile.

In the zoo there is a zebra
Who likes a zookeeper called Debra.
There is a giraffe who is very daft
But is very good at craft.

Thomas Croly (11)
St Joseph's RC Primary School, Heywood

The Dog

As dog's eyes
Peer over skies,
Legs are stable
Nothing can disturb them,
Velvet ears sway with fear,
Listens for the sound of tears.

Tails wagging,
Life's dragging,
Body shaking,
While digesting.

Dalmatians,
Alsatians,
Which one should I choose?
I bet they'll always chew my shoes!

Laura Hutchinson (10)
St Joseph's RC Primary School, Heywood

Chain Guys

Sunrise brings
Morning light,
Parents watch
Daily news,
Eating toast,
Jam too,
Go to school,
Go to work,
Have dinner,
Finish work,
Pick up kids,
Walk home,
Cook dinner.

Tomorrow you've got to do it all again!

Jade Mullen (10)
St Joseph's RC Primary School, Heywood

Water

Summer -
Cooling, refreshing,
Sparkling, glistening.

Autumn -
Full of leaves,
Shallow, chilling.

Winter -
Ice, snow, frozen,
Chilled to the bone.

Spring -
Fast-flowing, clean,
Reflecting, dripping
Water flowing down the river.

Darren Parker (11)
St Joseph's RC Primary School, Heywood

Darkness

As darkness falls over the land,
Trees are casting shadows onto the ground,
Moon lighting the water in the blue mist,
Seeing nothing but fog,
Everything dark and dull,
Headlights on,
Let's drive onwards,
Fog clearing,
Shadows disappearing,
Dawn awakening,
Clouds clearing,
Finally the sunlight comes.

Christopher Wroe (11)
St Joseph's RC Primary School, Heywood

Dolphins

D o not bite
O h so sweet
L oving animals
P retty cute
H appy animals
I t makes me happy
N ever will let me down
S ooooo playful!

Dolphins are everlasting friends
They will be forever there
Dolphins are sooooo cute
Dolphins, dolphins, swimming so deep
Play with me until I sleep.

Catherine Keane (11)
St Joseph's RC Primary School, Heywood

The Lion

Sandy fur,
Shining in the sun,
Going for camouflage,
Ready to pounce on its prey.

Animals trying to run, hide,
But there's no escaping.
The lion, sharp teeth,
Sharp claws,
Attacking its prey.
Fierce like a shark
Attacking a seal,
In the deep blue sea.

Aaron Brown (11)
St Joseph's RC Primary School, Heywood

Ponies

Ponies are very furry,
They have soft fur.
Most ponies are gentle,
Some are tame.
Ponies are sometimes friendly,
The good thing is . . .
They take you for rides,
They can be so clean,
If you wash them outside.

Ponies are kind of fun,
They are so playful,
Ponies are colourful,
They are so cute and don't smell,
You should think of getting one.

Rebecca Butler (10)
St Joseph's RC Primary School, Heywood

Thunder And Lightning

Rumbling, tumbling through the night
Scaring children with a fright
Banging and crashing through the air
Even scaring a grizzly bear
Setting off cannons with a boom
Look out everyone!
For the evil doom is upon you!
Fires flashing very bright
Still scaring children with a fright
Is it a ghost? So horribly frightening!
No, it's the old pals
Thunder and lightning!

Dominic Briddon (10)
St Joseph's RC Primary School, Heywood

The Ghost Boy

One day I was walking by the pond
And here appeared the ghost boy,
He arose swiftly from the water,
Holding his legendary ghost toy.

He spoke to me so timidly,
'Hello,' he kindly said,
'Hello,' I answered and boldly adding,
'What's that on your head?'

He said, 'That's where they shot me,
It was very near the brain.'
I said, 'Was it painful?'
But then he went insane.

The ghost tried to attack me,
But he and I both knew,
That he couldn't really hurt me,
But I ran and lost my shoe.

The shoe just fell off my foot,
So I hid behind a tree,
The ghost boy kicked it in the pond,
But he didn't look for me.

Dean Smith (11)
St Joseph's RC Primary School, Heywood

The Great Oak Tree

The great oak tree
Grows each day and night
Huge, round, soaring
Reaching to the sky
Reaches everlasting sea
The oak tree makes people resemble ants
The people make the tree resemble skyscrapers
Majestic oak tree, monument to eternity.

Chenise Fulton (11)
St Joseph's RC Primary School, Heywood

England Is Fantastic

England is fantastic,
It's full of pies and chips,
The food here is so fatty,
It builds around your hips.

England is fantastic,
It's full of football clubs,
The football's so exciting,
Great numbers watch in pubs.

England is fantastic,
It's full of glorious beer,
Sometimes it has a bad effect
And some people turn quite queer.

Nathan McGuinness (11)
St Joseph's RC Primary School, Heywood

Lions

There are lions in the jungle
Big, ferocious lions
With teeth like sharks
Running like cheetahs
And can climb trees
They are the kings of the jungle

You can only find them in Africa
If you hunt them
It will be a failure
Because they will eat you
If you wanted to catch one
You would have to be camouflaged.

Daniel Fleming (10)
St Joseph's RC Primary School, Heywood

Hallowe'en

Hallowe'en, the spooky night
Imagine having no light,
All the spiders, bugs that bite,
Secret witches flying around,
I bet they're even underground.

A full moon I see,
Oh look! People full of glee,
The night smoothingly goes by,
Witches fly.

You see cats' eyes glowing,
In a house you could see
A granny sewing,
There stands suddenly,
A witch with a wicked smile.

Lauren Bond (11)
St Joseph's RC Primary School, Heywood

Sunrise, Sunset

The sun is rising in the sky,
An early, sunny day.
Its hot flames reaching high,
Sun, please don't go away!

With a warming glow, ever so bright,
Blinding in every way.
You couldn't see a more beautiful sight,
Sun, please don't go away!

Sun, don't lose your heat,
It's now the afternoon.
There's the night you have to defeat,
Sun, please don't give way to the moon!

Bethany Krauza (11)
St Joseph's RC Primary School, Heywood

Brandi

I woke up one Christmas morning
and rushed to see what was there.
On the kitchen floor it sat,
it might bite but I didn't care.

Now I own a beautiful puppy,
she's ginger, brown and white.
Every time she runs in the wind,
her ears act like a kite.

She's small, furry and very cute,
you couldn't find a better dog.
She can be lazy but sometimes active,
every time I take her for a jog.

She gives me brilliant companionship,
she's with me all the time.
I'm glad I got her that Christmas morning,
that's why I'm writing this rhyme.

Chantelle McDowall (11)
St Joseph's RC Primary School, Heywood

The Cake

There once was a cake
that loved to bake
all different kinds of food
but it didn't know how
to bake a cow
who was in a very bad mood.

'Come here!' said the cake
'Or else I'll fetch my rake!'
And the cow immediately obeyed
it suddenly ran
and fell in the cake's pan
and soon a cow pie was made!

Gregory Weir (11)
St Joseph's RC Primary School, Heywood

Once Upon A Rhyme!

Once upon a rhyme,
Long ago in time,
Was a man called Jim,
Who lived in the land of Tim,
He chuckled *he he*
And jumped for joy *te te*,
With a laugh and a whistle,
He jumped into a thistle,
He screamed *argh argh!*
And shouted *tar! Tar'*
With a tumble and a bump,
He landed in a dump . . .
Once upon a rhyme!

Sophie Crewe (11)
St Joseph's RC Primary School, Heywood

Night

Witching hours, watching in the cold breeze
Ice fingers melting down your back
Moonlight shining on shadowy figures
Stars twinkling in blue darkness
Blurred shadows stealing
Cats' eyes gleaming
Figures dancing in a touch of mist
Footsteps following
Animals watching in foggy weather
Black clouds reflect sparkling moonlight
Watch out!
Night-time is for everybody to stay out of magic world.

Amy Davenport (11)
St Joseph's RC Primary School, Heywood

The Sea

The sea rolls in and out,
Often calm, sometimes rough,
It's always there without a doubt.
Sometimes, it's tough,
When I'm at the sea,
I feel pebbles,
I feel just like me,
I make some bubbles.
When I go, it's always sunny,
I quickly rush to the sea,
My cousin is sometimes funny,
I shout out, 'Yippee!'
When I've been in the sun,
I realised it was so much fun!

Natalie Duffy (11)
St Joseph's RC Primary School, Heywood

My Little Wart

My little wart makes me so proud
It makes me stand out in the crowd
It hurts a little
But it's very brittle
It sits on my nose
Just striking a pose
It hardly moves
And when it does, it really grooves
My little wart makes me so proud
It makes me stand out in the crowd.

Grace Murphy (11)
St Joseph's RC Primary School, Heywood

Dog Haikus

Animals are great
They're the best thing in the world
Especially dogs

Dogs need exercise
They like to eat meat and bones
They like to play fetch

Dogs are really cute
They can act fierce at the vets
Dogs are cruel to cats

Dogs grow very big
They like to play which is great
They are lovely pets!

Suzanne Blyzniuk (11)
St Joseph's RC Primary School, Heywood

The Man From Spain

The man from Spain
was a real pain,
he always moans
and always groans.

The man from Spain,
had a very big plane,
he always flew it,
but once he nearly blew it.

The man from Spain
had a wife called Jane,
she always shouted,
which the man never doubted.

Thomas McGeown (11)
St Joseph's RC Primary School, Heywood

The Sea

The sea
Always there
Sometimes calm, sometimes ferocious,
Sometimes consuming.
Like a child trying to reach his toy,
But always being pulled back by its mother.
It makes me full of regret for the sea
As it struggles across the rocks all day long
The sea
Reminds us how lucky we are.

Callum Murphy (11)
St Joseph's RC Primary School, Heywood

Survivor

I'm a survivor
I lost my fiver
Got on a bus
Beat out the puss
Of the driver's wart
But then I thought
All I want is this:
A wish!

Ryan Dolan (11)
St Joseph's RC Primary School, Heywood

Pets

We own pets,
They cost a lot of money,
People buy them because they are cute,
Others because they're funny.

Emily Peplow (11)
St Joseph's RC Primary School, Heywood

I'm A Veggie Human!

I'm a veggie human,
I've given up all meat,
I've given up all talking,
All I do is sing *tweet-tweet.*

I never, ever sink my teeth
Into some animal's skin,
It only lets the blood rush out
And lets the germs run in.

I used to be harmful,
I've even tried to kill!
But the sight of all that flesh,
Made me feel quite ill.

I once attacked a butterfly,
I sprang straight at its head,
I woke up three weeks later,
In a strange hospital bed.

Now I just eat carrots,
They're easier to kill,
Cos when I try to cook them
They all remain quite still!

Katie Beese (11)
St Joseph's RC Primary School, Heywood

My Next-Door Neighbour's Dog

My next-door neighbour's dog,
It wees all over my garden,
Smelly, loud and dirty,
It's like a barking machine,
It's like a magnet to my sister,
It makes me have a headache.
It's like the radio on full blast,
My next-door neighbour's dog,
Reminds me of how annoying life is.

Nicole Sacker (11)
St Joseph's RC Primary School, Heywood

Chantelle!

Chantelle is ever so groovy
And one day could be in a movie,
She can also be loud
And always loves a crowd,
She is always funky and
Fools around like a monkey.

Her favourite flower is a daisy
And is always acting crazy,
Her favourite pet is a dog
And her least favourite pet is a frog,
Chantelle is ever so groovy
And one day could be in a movie,
So all in all I would like to say,
Chantelle is a great friend in every way!

Bethany Jacques (11)
St Joseph's RC Primary School, Heywood

It's Not Fair

It's not fair,
Why can't I play football
Or ride a horse,
Climb a mountain,
Boil an egg?
Anything's better
Than doing a poem!

It's not fair,
Why can't I do stunts,
Play games,
Join the circus?
Anything's better
Than writing poems!

Nathan Kent (11)
St Joseph's RC Primary School, Heywood

My Sister, Bailie!

My sister, Bailie is such a show-off
Which really gets on my nerves,
She's fierce, evil and so big-headed,
She's like a pain in the neck
That won't go away.
Bailie is like the devil princess,
She can be so kind when she wants to be,
But most of the time she is incredibly nasty.
I feel like a pan boiling over,
Every time she's mean to me.
My sister Bailie is the biggest liar I know,
Which makes me so angry to kill.
Bailie makes me want to scream,
With her sharp nails and very long hair,
If I don't stop now I could really go on forever!

Erin Seabright (11)
St Joseph's RC Primary School, Heywood

The China Man

There once was a man from China
Who wasn't a very good climber
He slipped on a rock
And got quite a shock
As he landed on a shipyard dock!

Matthew Brooks (11)
St Joseph's RC Primary School, Heywood

Angels

Angels watching down from Heaven,
Sitting on clouds filled with pride,
They sit on chairs around small tables
While tucking into meals of bread and of rye.

Sarah Dickson (11)
St Joseph's RC Primary School, Heywood

A Bowl Of Jelly

Jelly is wobbly
It's nice to eat
It's hard to make
But so what?
It's a treat
It's cold to make
It's lovely
It turns to solid from the watery liquid
Smells so nice
I'd like to drink it when watery
Different colours
To do strawberry, red as blood
Lemon, it is yellow
As the sun
Raspberry is
Purple like a grape
Jellies are so nice but don't have a price.

Andrew Liley (11)
St Joseph's RC Primary School, Heywood

The Fierce Tiger

Bloodthirsty, merciless, untamed
Predator of the jungle
Heir to the sabre tooth
The tiger like a chameleon
Camouflaging itself into its
Surroundings
Like a deer sprinting for survival
I feel fearful like a rabbit
Entranced by a snake.

Stephen Ramotowski (10)
St Joseph's RC Primary School, Heywood

View Of An Elephant

A tree stomper
A gigantic creature
A poacher hater
A strong squirter
A noise machine
A wrinkly mammal
A gallomphing giant
A footprint maker.

Leoni Stanton (11)
St Joseph's Catholic Primary School, Wrightington

A View Of A Kitten

A ball of fluff
A furry friend
A milk drinker
A stripy fur ball
A slow runner
A mouse eater
A bird eater.

Katie Garner (10)
St Joseph's Catholic Primary School, Wrightington

View Of A Whale

A sea giant
A plankton gobbler
A tail waver
A water pistol
A loud speaker
A mysterious glider.

Emily Power (10)
St Joseph's Catholic Primary School, Wrightington

View Of A Tiger

A zebra's nightmare,
A stripy predator,
A man eater,
A fierce fighter,
A speedy sprinter,
A jungle inhabiter,
A dozing fluff ball,
A misunderstood cat.

Heather Thomas (11)
St Joseph's Catholic Primary School, Wrightington

View Of A Rat

A flea-ridden rodent,
A despised mouse,
A sewer inhabiter,
A garbage gobbler,
A human's enemy,
A cat's prey,
An attic invader,
The plague causer.

Hannah Ellis (11)
St Joseph's Catholic Primary School, Wrightington

A View Of A Falcon

A fast fighter
A mountain dominator
A fierce predator
A feather preener
A swift swooper
A sky diver
A brave flier.

Sam Pepper (11)
St Joseph's Catholic Primary School, Wrightington

My Family

My family and my cousins are fun
One of my youngest cousins has a fake gun
Although I have lots of cousins that drive me up the wall
I was playing with one and he made me fall
I have parents that are funny
I still have a hutch 'cause I used to have a bunny
My sister likes to play out
My cousin, Niamh, likes to shout
Daniel loves the Incredible Hulk
Eleanor puts on a fake sulk
I have to hamsters and two cats
In the night come out bats
I have a younger cousin called Lizzie
I have a second cousin that is busy, busy, busy
I have an uncle, Mike
I have a teddy dog called Spike.

Rachael Power (8)
St Joseph's Catholic Primary School, Wrightington

My Family Are Great

My mum goes to the shops
And buys all different kinds of pops,
My brother goes to school
And he thinks he's pretty cool,
My sister has homework
And she has a pig called Perk,
My dad has a pair of shades,
And has two maids.
Me, I like climbing our tree.

Alice Northey (8)
St Joseph's Catholic Primary School, Wrightington

View Of A Bear

A fierce mauler
A vicious fur ball
A deer hunter
A fishy fisher
A raging bull
A deer devourer
A roaring beast
A man eater.

Ben Logan (10)
St Joseph's Catholic Primary School, Wrightington

View Of A Cat

A fluffy ball
A fun friend
A cotton chaser
A mouse hunter
A lazy leaper
A meat eater
A tiny tiger
A cushion cuddler.

Jessica Nicholson (10)
St Joseph's Catholic Primary School, Wrightington

View Of A Leopard

A hungry predator,
A muscley runner,
A prey to lions,
A fierce eater,
A lazy cat,
A deer chaser,
A low croucher.

Joe Taylor (10)
St Joseph's Catholic Primary School, Wrightington

A View Of A Frog

A tongue zapper
A fly flicker
A pond jumper
A lily pad rocker
A French's prey
An egg layer
A spider's helper
A rainforest leaper
A balloon blower
A hopping horror
A magnificent croaker
A rough reptile.

Catherine Sayer (11)
St Joseph's Catholic Primary School, Wrightington

View Of An Ostrich

A fast runner
A big bird
A vicious pecker
A mad eater
A fluffy bird
A big beak.

Matthew Smith (11)
St Joseph's Catholic Primary School, Wrightington

View Of A Crocodile

A vicious snapper
A good spy
A pretend cry
A fast swimmer
A mean green fighting machine
A dirty eater.

Ryan Stevens (11)
St Joseph's Catholic Primary School, Wrightington

View Of A Lion

A muscly fur ball
A camouflaged creature
A vicious seeker
A fierce predator
A large cat
A deer's nightmare
The king of the jungle.

Zoe Crompton (10)
St Joseph's Catholic Primary School, Wrightington

View Of A Sheep

A grass nibbler
A soft cloud
A woolly jumper
A wolf's dinner
A farmer's friend
And people's friend
And your friend too.

Oliver McDonald (11)
St Joseph's Catholic Primary School, Wrightington

View Of A Cat

A fluff ball
A mouse hunter
A purring pest
A food waster
Attention lover
A lovable friend.

Mark Hill (10)
St Joseph's Catholic Primary School, Wrightington

Shark!

A water glider
A born predator
A sneaky adversary
A life taker
A killing machine
A water breather
A blood drinker
A meat eater
A seal devourer
A water liver
A young raiser
A killing warrior
A sly predator
A boat crasher.

Liam Kaye (11)
St Joseph's Catholic Primary School, Wrightington

View Of A Koala

A tree clinger
A quiet bug eater
A fuzzy fluff ball
A slow swinger
A fruit scavenger
An eucalyptus creeper.

Hannah Safaric (10)
St Joseph's Catholic Primary School, Wrightington

View Of A Bull

A drink
A horny cow
A red attacker
A grass-eating monster
A bull-riding terror.

Daniel Box (10)
St Joseph's Catholic Primary School, Wrightington

Nightmares

N ightmares are scary
I n my bed I see an evil fairy
G hosts and goblins creeping into my bed
H ear the witch come into my shed
T onight and tomorrow night they'll come again
M onsters and giants in the pouring rain
A nd in the morning the dreams are gone
R ise and shine
E verything is forgotten again.

James Clow (9)
St Mary's Catholic Primary School, Chorley

Dreams

D reams are hopes and aspirations
R eally exciting or really scary
E nd in the morning when Mum wakes you up
A nd sometimes you might find true love
M ums always finish the dream
    By shaking you right and left
S o have a good night's sleep
    And don't let the bedbugs bite.

Catherine Goulden (10)
St Mary's Catholic Primary School, Chorley

Dreams

D reams are funny
R eally funny
E xactly funny
A mazingly funny
M uch too funny to sleep.

Peter Cooper (11)
St Mary's Catholic Primary School, Chorley

Sweet Dreams!

A dream comes to you at night
Or defines your goal in life
In my dreams . . .
I want to be Venus Williams
I want to be the Queen
I want to sing in America
I want to live on ice cream
A smile on everyone's faces
A chance for worldwide peace
A house made out of chocolate
Sweet dreams are thoughts like these!

Lucinda Sparrow (11)
St Mary's Catholic Primary School, Chorley

My Dream Is To Be . . .

I dream of being an actress,
Stealing all of the stage,
In pantomimes and theatre,
The best one of my age.
It's just a dream today,
But tomorrow I will be,
An award winning actress
By the Mediterranean sea.

Rosalie Taylor (11)
St Mary's Catholic Primary School, Chorley

Dreams

My dream would be to meet my favourite pop star
And go for a ride in a brand new sports car
But I know that will never come true
But if I wait, it might be a dream that I will do.

Hannah Daniels (10)
St Mary's Catholic Primary School, Chorley

Nightmare!

I had a nightmare last night,
A really, really scary one,
I had a nightmare last night,
It was about monsters and ghosts,
I had a nightmare last night,
A really, really scary one,
I had a nightmare last night,
It was about dragons and knights,
I had a nightmare last night,
A really, really scary one,
I had a nightmare last night . . .

Rachel Wright (10)
St Mary's Catholic Primary School, Chorley

My Matrix Dream

Running through the shadows
Jumping off tall trees
I thought I'd learnt tai chi
Running on the sea
Sliding on carpets
Slicing up a rug
Flying in the air
'Scott, get up!'

Scott Pritchard (11)
St Mary's Catholic Primary School, Chorley

Dreams

My dream was a bad dream,
There was an ugly monster squirting me with cream,
It was big and hairy,
Moving just like a fairy
And it was coming to get me.

Jonathan Mather (9)
St Mary's Catholic Primary School, Chorley

My Awful Nightmare

I had a nightmare last night,
It gave me an awful fright,
It was about a killer who killed my mother,
He tried to kill me but he killed my brother,
I tried to get away but he was too fast,
I wondered if I would ever last,
Then it was morning, a really bright day,
I didn't know whether he would make me pay,
I went into my mum's room, to my delight . . .
No one was dead at all, it was just an awful fright.

Katie Imrie (11)
St Mary's Catholic Primary School, Chorley

Anywhere!

I can take you anywhere
To the zoo for a scare!
All the way up to the moon!
Back again for lunch at noon!
Sometimes I can make you glad
But sometimes I can make you sad.
What am I?
A dream.

Laura Anton (10)
St Mary's Catholic Primary School, Chorley

The Night

The darkness breathes the icy wind into little children's beds,
It edges its way around the world
Whilst the glimmering moon slips silently through the poisonous sky,
The shadows creep across the pure black sky.

Travis Noblett (11)
St Mary's Catholic Primary School, Chorley

Fantasy Dreams

Sleep is good
Dreams are better
Dreaming of rain
Is even wetter

Dreaming of flight
Soar through the night
Swim with fish . . .
Then eat them with chips!

Andrew Tierney (11)
St Mary's Catholic Primary School, Chorley

My Best Ever Dream

My best dream is being a motocross rider,
Whizzing over jumps and flying like a glider,
Coming first around the motocross track,
Never even thinking of looking back,
With some hope these dreams will come true
And remember people, I'll be thinking of you.

Lee Holt (11)
St Mary's Catholic Primary School, Chorley

I Wish I Was . . .

I wish I was a fish sipping gin
    going high into the sky

I wish I was a Ferrari Maranello
    flying through the streets

I wish I was a bird as well
    flying through the cold sky

Until my dad woke me up in the morning . . .

Jordan Murphy (10)
St Mary's Catholic Primary School, Chorley

Am I Famous?

Dreams are scary,
Dreams give you a fright,
Dreams give you a fright,
In the middle of the night.

But this dream was not scary,
This dream did not give me a fright,
It didn't give me a fright
In the middle of the night,
This dream was famous.

The fame that travelled through my mind,
The fans that had come, I could not find,
Where are they?
I searched high and low,
Now I will never know,
If I am famous or not.

Kelly Wallwork (10)
St Mary's Catholic Primary School, Chorley

My Dream

I want to be famous
I want to be rich
That is my wish

Every night I have the same dream
I never dream about flowers or streams
I try but I just cannot

Maybe when I step outside
There will be flashes
There will be masses of people

This is my dream!

Emily Hargreaves (11)
St Mary's Catholic Primary School, Chorley

My Best Dream

Me and my brother were in the war,
We would never surrender,
We fought all night,
Until it was light
And soon we had victory,
I left with a medal,
And I was . . . 'Liam, get up!
You are going to be late for school.'
'OK Mum,' I said throwing the covers off me.

Liam Delaney (10)
St Mary's Catholic Primary School, Chorley

Dreams

D reams are good but sometimes bad,
R eal or not they are
E lectrifying, exciting, bad or sad
A nother world afar,
M y dream might be mad but I'm glad,
S o many dreams come true.

Lindsey Flux (11)
St Mary's Catholic Primary School, Chorley

Vampire Nightmare

D racula will come
R ed the colour of his meal
E veryone beware
A lways he moves
M oving in the shadows
S hadows of your dreams . . .

Danny Mercer (11)
St Mary's Catholic Primary School, Chorley

What Dreams Are Like

Dreams are great, dreams are cool
When you're chilling by the pool
Dreams are scary, dreams are creepy
When you're falling very sleepy
Dreams are silly, dreams are ace
When you see a funny face
But when you wake up
It all goes away
Hopefully it will come back another day.

Jamie Goodman (10)
St Mary's Catholic Primary School, Chorley

My Dream

I dream I am in a Ferrari, driving down Monaco
And I'm in first place racing down,
But suddenly I lose control and all the other racing cars
Get in front of me,
Brum! Brum!
As they zoom past me,
'Wakey-wakey! We're going to watch the race at Monaco.'

Samuel Fishwick (10)
St Mary's Catholic Primary School, Chorley

The Dream Of Chorley!

There was an old dream of Chorley,
That took over and made everyone poorly,
It made everybody sad,
But very bad,
That horrible dream of Chorley.

Oliver Lee (11)
St Mary's Catholic Primary School, Chorley

Nightmares Of The Century

One night I thought about a scary house
The biggest house in the world
And standing there like a little mouse
My hair all furled and curled

A monster came to that scary house
And he scared me away
And all alone like that little mouse
I'm afraid I'd have to say

I ran and ran without a warning
So I collapsed on somebody's bed
And I found out when I woke up the next morning
It was all just a dream in my head!

Danielle Troake (11)
St Mary's Catholic Primary School, Chorley

Last Night I Had A Fright

Last night I had a fright
I awoke in the middle of the night
A lot of big and scary monsters
Big and very hairy
It kept me awake all night
I got a very big fright.

Alexander Straw (10)
St Mary's Catholic Primary School, Chorley

Dreams

My dream is to live in a mansion,
I know it won't come true,
But if I wait, it might just happen,
So I'll keep on dreaming.

Ruth Evans (10)
St Mary's Catholic Primary School, Chorley

Monster Madness

Lying in bed alone at night
Darkness creeping inwards
Monster slinking round my room
Grumbling bellies with them
Striding closer mouths wide open
Coming right for me
Sweat is dripping off my body
They want me for their tea
Closer, closer, bending over
Whatever can I do?
'Wake up, lazy bones
Get up, it's time to go
Monsters to see
Things go do
In museum for monsters
Let's go!'

Ania Neisser (11)
St Mary's Catholic Primary School, Chorley

Haikus

The stream running past
Fishes jumping in and out
Small boats sailing by

The birds are singing
I am playing and laughing
Sweetly the sun sets

Rolling on the grass
Relaxing in the cold stream
I breathe in pure air.

Charlotte Flanagan (9)
St Mary's Catholic Primary School, Chorley

Who Am I?

I take over you in class
Just when you get bored

I help you to sleep at night

I can eat you
So you better watch out

When your mum calls
Cornflakes are ready

I go back to sleep.

Matthew Wilson (11)
St Mary's Catholic Primary School, Chorley

The Dream I Nearly Had For The Whole Night!

I had a nightmare,
A scary nightmare,
It was about ghosts
And monsters above me,
They were getting closer,
I was so scared, I was . . .
Awake in the flash of a light!

Jessica Clitheroe (11)
St Mary's Catholic Primary School, Chorley

Haikus

Cold winds, soft snowfall,
frosty white snow trickling down
softly on the ground.

Sparrows fluttering
in the icy cold bare trees.
Hungry and freezing.

Helena Kelly (8)
St Mary's Catholic Primary School, Chorley

My Dream Is To Be . . .

M y dream is to climb the highest mountain,
Y ou and me to swim through the biggest fountain.

D reaming about climbing all the way to Heaven,
R emembering the time when I lost my way in Devon,
E xtremely excited about standing up high,
A ll the way up into the starry sky,
M y dream is to be the *best!*

Catherine Richardson (11)
St Mary's Catholic Primary School, Chorley

Holidays!

H appy people,
O n the beach,
L ying on the soft, smooth sand,
I n the sea the fish swim by,
D olphins jumping up to the sky
A nd so the sun gradually sets,
Y ellow moon comes up from its rest.

Katie Farley (9)
St Mary's Catholic Primary School, Chorley

Holidays!

H appy days have come again,
O h! How happy can it be
L ying in the sun?
I n the sea the fishes swim,
D olphins diving skilfully,
A long the beach the children play,
Y ellow sun shines brightly.

Daniel Forshaw (8)
St Mary's Catholic Primary School, Chorley

Holidays!

H urry, school has nearly ended,
O ver the holidays I've planned,
L ying in the steaming hot sun,
I dream of the rest of the time to come.
D ays together with my friends,
A lthough this fun will soon come to an end,
Y ellow sun will come again.

Joseph Ellison (8)
St Mary's Catholic Primary School, Chorley

Holidays!

H appy faces smiling on the beach,
O n the beach we have room to play,
L et's just sit and stay all day,
I n the pools ,I see a starfish,
D ay after day I feel so glad I came,
A t night I dream of sand and sea,
Y esterday was just you and me.

Danny Harty (9)
St Mary's Catholic Primary School, Chorley

Dreams

D reams are running round my head,
R unning round in my bed,
E very night I sit awake,
A t the park, in the lake,
M y mum shouts up for me,
S till I am in a dream, up, awake with an ice cream.

Scott Whittle (10)
St Mary's Catholic Primary School, Chorley

Dreams

One night I lay in bed
And on the pillow I lay my head
Closed my eyes and started to snore . . .

I went to my gran one evening
(I had just been weeping)
'Gran?' I said scared
I looked at her but there was no one there

I ran all over my house
But there was just me and my mouse
I screamed so loud the mirrors cracked
And someone upstairs laughed

I ran upstairs and looked in the bathroom
Mr Hyde, my worst enemy, I was doomed
Someone help me, someone please
He pulled out his gun and aimed at me . . .

'Wake up Pops, now'
I woke up and my sisters were having a row
'Time for school,' my mum said, 'and pipe down you two'
I tried to hold on to my dream but I couldn't remember if it's true.

Poppy Aldridge (10)
St Mary's Catholic Primary School, Chorley

Haikus

The stream running past
Sweet birds singing in the trees
Blue fishes swim by

Water to swim in
Yummy picnic to munch on
The sun is shining.

Rebecca Linfitt (8)
St Mary's Catholic Primary School, Chorley

Dreams

Dreams are exciting, dreams are wild,
Daydreams and nightmares go through every child,
Ghost and goblins may haunt you at night,
Daydreams that you fall off a steep height,
Nightmares may come around like bats,
Witches will come with their wicked cats.

Daydreams, nightmares, hopes and aspirations!
Daydreams, nightmares, hopes and aspirations!

Can't get the thoughts out of my head,
They come mostly when I'm in bed.
Fluffy pillows, cotton clouds,
What more do you want than screaming crowds?
Spaceships and rockets shooting into space,
I think dreaming is totally ace!

Daydreams, nightmares, hopes and aspirations!
Daydreams, nightmares, hopes and aspirations!

Sam Wright (10)
St Mary's Catholic Primary School, Chorley

Dreams

When I was in bed,
I had a good dream,
When I was in bed,
I had a good dream.
I dreamt I was a pop star,
I loved driving round in my very posh car,
The pop star I am is Posh Spice,
I like my dream because it is nice,
Being a pop star is so great,
I will tell this dream to my mate.

Vikki Bowler (9)
St Mary's Catholic Primary School, Chorley

Scary

D reams are scary
R eally, really scary
E xtremely scary
A lways scary
M uch too scary
S cary!

Euan Dickson (11)
St Mary's Catholic Primary School, Chorley

The Shoot

A flutter of wings
A flying bird
A blast of a gun
A life has been taken

A mist of smoke
A talking voice
A bird's choke
The gunmen hear
A raised gun
A pull of a trigger
A dead bird, whose life has gone.

Thomas Holden (11)
St Mary's Hall School, Stonyhurst

Fire Haiku

Like a light bulb's glow
A raging crackling danger
A beautiful light.

Edward Courteney-Harris (11)
St Mary's Hall School, Stonyhurst

The Oily Ostrich

The
oily
ostrich
trudges
around,
with
nothing
to do,
not
making
a sound,
but when the night
comes and the sun
disappears,
the ostrich sneers
and leers
at its
owner who
watches for
an egg to appear.

Alexander Ahmed (10)
St Mary's Hall School, Stonyhurst

The Sky Is . . .

A blue ocean
Alive
A cloudy heaven
A picture
A river rapid
An everlasting space
A dolphin
A blanket of blue
A stormy sea
Forever changing.

Joshua Vines (11)
St Mary's Hall School, Stonyhurst

Unexpected Win

It was our kick-off
It was 44:46 to them
We needed another try

And it was five minutes to the end
We had kick-off
It was in the air
Forwards got there
Quickly
And won the ball
I was the winger
But I was meant to be a forward
It came quickly down the line
I had it
I ran and ran
Two boys were coming up like tigers
I dodged the two boys
Tackled on the try line
I was in the air
I was going for it!
I was right above the boy
I scored
We won
Yes
We had won.

James Gale (11)
St Mary's Hall School, Stonyhurst

Teacher

Cold, slender,
Eye upon,
Watching every move you make.

Tapping on the desk,
Doing maths, doing English,
Write away, no bother.

Grace Mercer (8)
St Mary's Hall School, Stonyhurst

WWE Wrestling

That day Goldberg beat Triple H with ease
And Triple H was a big bloody mess
And Lita came on in her purple dress
Shaun had won before he could even sneeze
Terjerry lets out gas like lots of bees
And The Undertaker runs on like a pest
On jumps Kane, puts The Undertaker to rest
Stone Cold enters, Terjerry begs, 'Please, please'

Then Brock Lesnar comes on and does F-five
And Triple H comes on and does the 'pedigree'
Big Evil comes on and does a dive
That lovely day, the matches were all free
We sat at the ringside and felt alive
Our hero won and that pleased Walt and me!

Matthew Bond (11)
St Mary's Hall School, Stonyhurst

Nature

Nature is wonderful and beautiful,
The forest is covered with small bluebells.
The wet bark of dark trees gives lovely smells,
The forest is so sweet and wonderful.
The sea is a wild world but is harmful,
A diver has true stories that he tells
Of the deep depths where he can pick seashells,
The sea is calm, relaxing and is peaceful.

The sky is like cotton dipped in blue ink,
The sky sometimes lets the lightning come through,
The sky is like a blanket of blue silk,
The sky paints different colours like pink
And purple and orange, not always blue
And clouds are like a long cool glass of milk.

Victoria Welch (11)
St Mary's Hall School, Stonyhurst

A Dolphin

Through gleaming water fast and sleek and bright,
The swift blue dolphin weaves and dives and glides.
Through ocean's salt it rides on waves
And this is how it moves, a dolphin's flight.
While through ocean's hazards dolphins fight,
The dolphin sways through pollution's tide,
Currents are the dolphin's only guide,
The dolphin's chance of survival is slight.

The fisher hunts for food in his net,
The dolphin eyes up the newly caught fish,
A game to eat the fishes seems like play.
The fisher's catch is good as it can get,
For with the fish, the dolphin is held taut,
The seas have one less dolphin left today.

Peter Shorthouse (10)
St Mary's Hall School, Stonyhurst

Inside My Head There Is A Rainforest

Inside my head there is a rainforest,
The air is damp,
My skin is wet,
Sounds are spinning in my head,
It is hot and feels sticky,
Birds are bright and very pretty,
The trees are tall, the flowers bright,
So many different kinds in sight,
Many sounds echo through the forest,
Animals creeping in the undergrowth,
Snakes slither under the leaves,
Monkeys swing amongst the trees.

Dario Mastrobuoni
St Mary's Hall School, Stonyhurst

My Strange And Musical Pets

My family and I have a dog,
He is as thick as a log,
There is one thing that he is good at,
He is a musical dog,
Late in the night when the fires are out,
My dog comes galloping outside,
We try to stop him but instead of that,
We make him howl, so how is that?

And now for my cat,
She's as blind as a bat,
She doesn't even know where her bed is,
She creeps out at night
And gives people a fright,
By miaowing as loud as a jet,
My neighbours complain,
But they are insane,
Because she's a musical cat.

My budgie is mad,
Because she is sad,
As she groans
And moans,
The sky turns grey,
Because she is singing
A sad song every day.

My mysterious hamster
Is a full-time gangster,
Who robs from his room-mate, Fluffy,
I don't understand,
He gets all of his share,
But he's a greedy hamster.

Mary Ann Wootton (10)
St Mary's Hall School, Stonyhurst

My Little Menace

I have a little brother,
Who wipes his nose on my mother.
He's revolting you can say
In every single way, but
Wiping his nose on my mother,
He's just completely mad.

The other day
He ran through the house
With muddy shoes,
He ran upstairs
Shouting and screaming,
He ran through my bedroom
And tore my diary apart.

He sprayed my cat pink!
It did look quite nice
I have to say,
But I wasn't so happy
When he died the next day.

But when at night he settles down,
He's ever so sweet, the way he sleeps,
I forget the things he has done,
What I never realise is
How our friendship will fade away
As soon as I get older.

Megan Ansbro (10)
St Mary's Hall School, Stonyhurst

Half-Term

In the dorm the windows creak,
The door closes with a knock,
You count down every minute of every night,
In the class you look at the clock
And then the bell rings in your ear!
You jump up in joy - half-term has begun.

Hugo Noble (11)
St Mary's Hall School, Stonyhurst

All Alone

My older brother went away,
I never thought he would go,
I thought he would always be around,
He's in a different country now,
When he comes back, he's going in the army.

I don't want him to go,
I never did,
I never said so, though,
But deep in my heart,
I know he should go.

My sister will be next,
She's going in the army too,
I never say so,
But I love her so,
I don't want her to go.

She thinks I hate her,
But really I don't,
I love her just as much as my brother,
I don't want to let either of them go.

When my brother and sister go,
I'll be all alone,
I can't bear to think when that day will come,
You should be nicer to your family,
For you'll never know when they'll go.

Eleanor Russell-Blackburn (10)
St Mary's Hall School, Stonyhurst

She Doesn't Know

She doesn't know what to write
Because she's brainy and bright
But she looks out the window at night.

Darcy Coop (9)
St Mary's Hall School, Stonyhurst

Memories Remain

(Dedicated to my puppy, Nelson, I'll never forget him)

May the eighth
And December
Make me realise - remember
My one and only Labrador
He was black - him I adored

His silky fleece
His floppy ears
The day he went just brings back tears
But deep inside I know he's near
His wagging tail - his eyes so dear

And far away in a distant land
I know he's running with a leap and bound
The bark of his joy, an almighty sound
In Heaven's sweet autumn leaves, his love rings aloud.

Alice Eastwood (10)
St Mary's Hall School, Stonyhurst

The Bee

Beautiful queen,
Like a bird in the air,
Landing in such lonely ground so green,
Blossoming clouds so graceful, so fair,
She never worries nor has a care.

The flutters around frightening creatures,
But then *swat!*
She becomes nothing at all.

Maryum Ahmed (10)
St Mary's Hall School, Stonyhurst

The War In Iraq

Bush declared war in two thousand and three,
We went in and began to win the war.
The troops began to roll on land and air.
Hundreds of men have died, Iraq's now free.
The noose was tightened and the rat was caught,
It wasn't dead, but it was very weak.
Attacks on Basra go on as we speak,
The Shi'ite militant are being fought.

Bush kicked down the door, began the war,
The door is down. The war? It still goes on.
The Spanish ran out through the open door.
At the first sign of trouble they were gone.
Europe thinks the war has gone too far,
But I think we should stay, until it is done.

Charles Jolleys (11)
St Mary's Hall School, Stonyhurst

A Plane Poem

Off you go soaring up high
Right up into the sky
Eventually you level out
Staying straight not wandering about
Gliding through the air so light
Oh, what a glorious flight
Finally you have to descend
The flight has come to an end
You land with a gentle bump
And your passengers depart.

Eleanor Parker (10)
St Mary's Hall School, Stonyhurst

The Scourge Of Camelot

From Hell they came,
On fiery dragons they came,
The scourge of Camelot.

Bold warrior and knight,
Fell before them,
The scourge of Camelot.

'Camelot will never fall,'
Brave warrior shouted from the wall,
To the scourge of Camelot.

King Arthur with his sword,
For which he was crowned,
Shouted, 'Go back to Hell,'
Scourge of Camelot.

He raised his sword and with these words,
'Light with no boundary, come forth destroy,'
The scourge of Camelot.

The creatures fell back to Hell,
Evil vanquished and therefore fell,
The scourge of Camelot.

Jack Agnew (10)
St Mary's Hall School, Stonyhurst

The Bubble

The bubble,
Floating up or down,
So high in the air;
Its fate in the hand of the winds.
The children blowing it up or down,
The bubble seeing the whole world,
The beautiful world,
That's until its time comes
And it
Pops.

William Rowley (11)
St Mary's Hall School, Stonyhurst

Love

When I was twenty, young and new
Sitting in the corner blue
A word I saw floating round
Never falling to the ground
This word so big
That grew like figs
Is 'love'

Love, it said
I thought and stopped
Until it caused my mind to pop
This word I said
Has much to show
For it has caused my mind to blow
So bow to this great, beautiful dove
This giant, kingly thing called 'Love'.

Catriona Graffius (10)
St Mary's Hall School, Stonyhurst

My Dreams

My dreams are important
They make my wishes come true
And when I see and hear them
It makes me feel they are true.

    My dreams make me happy
    And sad too
    They mostly make me happy
    That's true, true, true.

My dreams make me imagine
That I have magical things
They make me excited
Because the bells ring.

Georgie Kelly (9)
St Mary's Hall School, Stonyhurst

A Penguin Poem

Waves crash,
Spray comes
Up and on the
Rock sits a penguin
He watches the
Choppy sea horses
In the rough sea
He dives deep
Down in freezing
Water to find his
Prey; for he shall
Have to eat today
His streamlined body
And webbed feet help
Manoeuvre him through
The water, he sees a fish
Towards it he races
Fast as a cheetah
And catches it in his
Bill, when back
On shore the penguin
Pecks at the raw
Fish
In
His beak.

Thomas Rowley (11)
St Mary's Hall School, Stonyhurst

My Sad Dad

My sad dad
Went fairly mad,
Then he went hyper
And put on a diaper.

The doctor said
He needs a new head,
Or else he'd go barmy
And take on the army.

He did exactly this
And gave my mum a kiss,
Then he drove a tank
And soon blew up the bank.

The general shouted, 'Stop!'
And took cover in a shop,
My dad turned from mad
Into just plain bad.

The army had to shoot
And it really made Dad scoot,
My dad ran but fell over,
The white cliffs of Dover.

Then to the general Dad said, 'Here!'
And offered him a beer,
So after a pint my dad was not bad, mad or even sad,
Just plain old Dad!

Peter Watts (10)
St Mary's Hall School, Stonyhurst

As We Look Down

Gliding through the air looking at the view
The fire burning our faces as we ascend to Heaven
We're at the top of the world - the wind in our hot faces
Looking at those patchwork quilts with shades of green, dark and light
As the fire goes out, we're not moving like a slug on sand
We're going down, everyone can see the balloon
The end of an adventure
Now we're the ants on the ground.

Maxwell Nelson (11)
St Mary's Hall School, Stonyhurst

A Kite

A kite blowing
High in the sky,
Waiting for the wind to die,
The bright blue sky
Waiting for the kite to
Go on swiftly in the sky,
Fighting, flying against the sky,
Blowing higher, higher,
Along the sky.

Philippa Layzell (11)
St Mary's Hall School, Stonyhurst

Butterfly

She lands in the grass
She is so beautiful
Just like a flower
She does not cower

Intently she seems to watch the rabbits
Gleefully she sees the bees making their honey
She will fly so high
She is the queen of the sky.

Lauren Reilly (11)
St Mary's Hall School, Stonyhurst

Dogs

What happiness a dog has,
With a tail and head,
It's the cutest animal I had,
What happiness a dog has.

What happiness a dog has,
Four feet and two eyes,
It's my favourite memories I have had.
What happiness a dog has.

Asmita Catherine Chitnis (9)
St Mary's Hall School, Stonyhurst

The Plane

The plane
Flies
Through the air, high in the sky
It glides and slides
Through the air
With the
Engines
Buzzing
Loud.

Joseph Reed (10)
St Mary's Hall School, Stonyhurst

What Is . . . A Dolphin?

A dolphin is a silky smooth leather coat,
Shining and glistening in the sun,
She dives and performs tricks for her audience,
A dolphin's long snout touches the tip of the sand,
All the fish make an archway for the fascinating creature.

Ashleigh Stewart (9)
St Patrick's School, Rochdale

What Is . . . The Moon?

The moon is a white chalk circle
on a piece of black card.

It is salt tipped onto a dark floor.

It is a blob of white paint
smudged on my navy school skirt.

It is a silver bouncy ball
bounced into the dark sky.

It is a grey pebble dropped
into the dirty pond.

Lauren Newsham (9)
St Patrick's School, Rochdale

What Is . . . A Turtle?

A turtle is a lily pad in the sea,
It is a creature in a seashell,
Its home doubles up as a hide-and-seek den
And it's a fish underwater,
A turtle is a dot in the sea,
It is a station for signs.

Kieren Iannidinardi (9)
St Patrick's School, Rochdale

The Giraffe

Its neck is a long snake.
Its colour is a banana with brown spots.
It eats leaves from the treetops.
Its tongue is sandpaper, long and rough.
It's gentle and agile, but strong and tough.

Emily Corcoran (10)
St Patrick's School, Rochdale

What Is . . . The Sea?

The sea is calm
It won't do any harm

The sea tastes of salt
A bit like malt

The waves are bad
And they are mad

They crash against the shore
And I sit on the moors.

Christopher Wawrzyn (10)
St Patrick's School, Rochdale

A Sheep

A sheep is a fluffy white cloud
that has fallen from the sky.

It is a woolly jumper
with a head and four legs.

It has a coat as soft
as two feather pillows.

Grace Rodgers (10)
St Patrick's School, Rochdale

What Is . . . A Guitar?

A guitar has three or four strings
And they go *ping, ping*
Guitars are big and they are small
But they can't come very, very tall
A guitar is like a big tennis racket
On it you can serve friendly music.

Alistair Goczan (9)
St Patrick's School, Rochdale

What Is . . . A Candle?

The flame of the candle dancing around everywhere
like a world class ballerina
The wax melting like a vanilla flavoured ice cream
The candle burns like a big hot fireball
The wax trickling down the sides of the candle like
people running down the road in the marathon
The flame shines like foil glittering in the moonlight
The candle is hard like clots of mud
clamped together
The flame is fluttering like people in an
aerobics class going forwards and backwards.

Megan Gillson & Reannon Lamb (10)
St Patrick's School, Rochdale

A Star

A star is a glistening chunk of gold
On a sheet of black silk
Floating in the sky

It's a gold star-shaped pin
On a piece of black card

A star is the golden sand
In a sea of black.

Samantha Purdy (10)
St Patrick's School, Rochdale

Dogs

A dog is a home pet
It has a collar with its name on
And likes to play a friendly game
It growls like heavy thunder
When it lets you stroke it, it feels silky soft
When it's in the bath, it smells like it's in a pool of roses.

Danielle Clarke (10)
St Patrick's School, Rochdale

What Is . . . A Loaf Of Bread?

A loaf of bread is a doughy cake
A soft cushion on a sofa

It is a cake
Burning in an oven

It is a golden rectangle
In a goldmine

It is a spongy cloth
Next to the tap

It is a waiting smell
When you open the bread bin.

Leigh Revilles (10)
St Patrick's School, Rochdale

What Are . . . Planets?

Planets are like tiny bouncy balls
being thrown around in the sky.

They are like a *hrrrrring* noise
moaning round the stratosphere.

They are like round balls of stone
being pelted round the Earth.

They are like coloured bonbons
floating above us.

They are like clumps of sand
being bowled around each other.

Kate Fisher (10)
St Patrick's School, Rochdale

The Magic Box

(Based on 'Magic Box' by Kit Wright)

I will put in my box . . .
The mane of a lion, soft and furry,
The voice of an angel, sweet and small,
The scent of wine, strong and sour.

I will put in my box . . .
The sound of a cat's cry,
The leaping flame of a bonfire,
The bouncing smell of a rose.

I will put in my box . . .
The last purr from a cat,
The third wish of a girl,
The first bark of a puppy.

I will put in my box . . .
The dry water from the sun,
The wet sand from a desert,
The light from the dark.

I shall use my box,
I will store my secrets,
I will lock up my love,
Tie up my fears.

Paige Ashworth (11)
St Patrick's School, Rochdale

What Is . . . A Rainbow?

A rainbow has colourful lines
mixed with different things like rain and sun

It is a semi-circle shape
with different colours you could all imagine

Right up in the sky
it is really long

It seems to go on forever . . .

Erin Grayson (10)
St Patrick's School, Rochdale

The Sea

The sea is a bath moving in the wind
making waves as it goes

The sea is a mass of clapping hands
after someone has performed

The sea is a jelly
wobbling on a plate

The sea is water
with a salty finish to it

The sea is seaweed
smelling of the sand from the shore above

The sea can be anything you want it to be.

Charlotte Watson (9)
St Patrick's School, Rochdale

Autumn Leaves

Autumn leaves have fallen on the lawn's wide dish,
At night and noon the wind a spoon that stirs them with a swish.
In the dish are thousands of crunchy, crispy, brown flakes,
You can smell the musky smell that the leaves make.
It now is the time for the leaves to go as we all know,
But we have something left, the sugar known as snow.

Erin Kenny (10)
St Patrick's School, Rochdale

What Is . . . The Sun?

The sun is a big yellow circle floating in the air.
It is a shiny star high in the air.
It is a bright red thumbprint on a pale pink sheet of paper.
It is a big orange smiley face without the eyes, the nose and the lips.
It is a shiny gold earring, very big and in the sky.

Ciara Rafter (10)
St Patrick's School, Rochdale

My Poem

(Based on 'Magic Box' by Kit Wright)

I will put in my box . . .
The beautiful blue sky
And the cheerful green grass splashing about

I will put in my box . . .
The colourful sky

I will put in my box . . .
A grey telescope to watch over everyone
And a book to read

I will put in my box . . .
The swishing of the trees
The stillness of the leaves
And the multicoloured birds flying away.

Kyle George (11)
St Patrick's School, Rochdale

What Is . . . The Moon?

The moon is a piece of cheese
that has been caught in the sky.

It is a silver coin
dropped off a silver chain.

It is a white thumbprint
on a piece of black paper.

It is a grey ball
killing werewolves.

It is a silver cap off a bottle
that has been drowned by a puddle.

Joshua Tipler (10)
St Patrick's School, Rochdale

The Magic Box

(Based on 'Magic Box' by Kit Wright)

I will put in my box . . .
The purr of a kitten, soft and warm
The brightly-coloured feathers of a peacock's tail
The lush sound of a puppy's cry

I will put in my box . . .
The angelic voice of a mother singing
The soft touch of a child's face
The roaring thunder of playful children rushing down the stairs

I will put in my box . . .
The luscious taste of the last ever chocolate
The soft whippiness of a lovely ice cream
And the soft splashes of water against my feet

I will put in my box . . .
A fish in a tree
And a bird in the sea
The blue of the grass
And the green of the sky

My box is fashioned
From the reddest of roses
And fire and ice mixed together
Looks nice and it stands on sweeping silver stars

I shall travel in my box
Across the desert
Across the sea
And across the mountains
As high as can be.

Cathryn Gisicki (11)
St Patrick's School, Rochdale

The Magic Box

(Based on 'Magic Box' by Kit Wright)

I will put in my box . . .
The sweet sound of a kitten's purr,
A rainbow of brightly-coloured summer blossoms,
The soft touch of a Golden Labrador.

I will put in my box . . .
The gentleness of the white horses in the ocean,
A fluffy white cloud from the bright blue sky,
A glistening star from the darkness of the night.

I will put in my box . . .
The genie from Aladdin,
The sweetest smile of a young child,
The soft skin of a newborn baby.

I will put in my box . . .
The 13th month and the 4th side of a triangle,
A fish in a hole and a rabbit in the sea,
The yellow of the ocean and the blue of the sand.

My box is fashioned from
The finest of silver, candy-coated dreams
And sugar-filled fantasies,
With golden stars on the lid and secrets in the corners
And ice and fire as the hinges.

I shall travel the world in my box,
Across all the continents and through all the oceans,
Then wash ashore a beach the colour of the sun
And knowing that my journey is over
Leave all my fears behind.

Amy Johnson (11)
St Patrick's School, Rochdale

The Magic Box

(Based on 'Magic Box' by Kit Wright)

I will put in the box . . .
A patch of rabbit's finest fur
A cup of the freshest water from
The most beautiful water fountain,
A piece of the most freshest smelling piece of grass.

I will put in the box . . .
The most colourful feather from a peacock,
A bunch of the most sweetest smelling flowers
And a leaf from the most beautiful tree.

I will put in the box . . .
The softest piece of velvet,
The biggest wave in the ocean,
The finest petal off the prettiest flower.

I will put in the box . . .
The green of the sky,
The blue of the grass,
The yellow of the sea,
The blue of the sand.

My box is fashioned from jewels to shells,
With butterflies on the lid and patterns in the corners,
Dragons' tongues for hinges.

I shall swim in my box
In the deepest water,
Then climb out and go down the steps into
The largest, warmest jacuzzi all to myself.

Emily Barrow (10)
St Patrick's School, Rochdale

The Magic Box

(Based on 'Magic Box' by Kit Wright)

I will put in my box . . .
The smell of a fresh bun,
The smile of a relative,
The brightness of the sun.

I will put in my box . . .
The happiness of a dear friend walking through the door,
The scent of a flower,
The waves of the shore.

I will put in my box . . .
A gift for me,
A rainbow of dreams,
Honey from a bee.

I will put in my box . . ...
The green of the sky,
The blue of the grass,
Plus a walking fish and a swimming fly.

My box is fashioned with beautiful jewels,
Its sides are covered with sand,
The inside is full of all my possessions
And is the most beautiful box in the land.

I shall surf in my box,
I shall swim in the sea,
I shall touch the sun
In my box made for me.

Vicky Doolin (11)
St Patrick's School, Rochdale

The Magic Box!

(Based on 'Magic Box' by Kit Wright)

I will put in my box . . .
The smell of freshly-baked buns
A rainbow of dreams
The voice of an angel

I will put in my box . . .
The warmth of the beating sun
The sound of a whistling wind
The taste of the most exotic fruits

I will put in my box . . .
The sound of a child crying with laughter
The whisper of the sea
A shooting star bright as day

I will put in my box . . .
A smile from a relative
The shiniest moon you've ever seen
The silky velvet from my pillow

I will put in my box . . .
A wing of a flower
A petal of a dove

My box will be fashioned from
The shiniest seashells
The most beautiful flowers
And completed with colourful patterns

My box has a brass lock on the front.

Hayley Duckworth (11)
St Patrick's School, Rochdale

The Magic Box!

(Based on 'Magic Box' by Kit Wright)

I will put in my box . . .
The growl of a tiger cub, young and strong,
A rainbow of roses, red as blood,
The scent of many perfumes.

I will put in my box . . .
The chirping of my pet budgerigar,
A sip of fruits from the most exotic,
The moon so bright from the dark sky.

I will put in my box . . .
The loud scream of a hostage,
The first word of a baby,
The first of many musical tunes.

I will put in my box . . .
The blue of the sun, the yellow of the sky,
The howl of an owl, the hoot of a wolf,
A dolphin in a cage, a bird in the sea.

My box is fashioned from
Silver and gold, only the shiniest, I have been told,
Big shells from the sandiest beaches,
The prettiest flowers from the biggest bouquet.

I shall surf in my box
On the bright blue waves,
Then glide ashore to the yellow sandy beach,
The reflection of the sun in the sea.

Now I shall close my magic box!

Leonie Richardson (11)
St Patrick's School, Rochdale

The Magic Box

(Based on 'Magic Box' by Kit Wright)

I will put in my box . . .
The lapping of water on a golden shore,
The excitement of a puppy, waiting to explore,
The oriental music of eastern China,
The most beautiful rose, there is none finer.

I will put in my box . . .
The dream of floating on a cloud,
A *scream* which is so very loud,
A garden of flowers,
Supernatural powers.

I will put in my box . . .
The coldest piece of ice,
The smallest of mice,
A friend that always plays,
A hen that never lays.

I will put in my box . . .
A flower from a coin
And change from a seed,
A hand that wears a shoe
And a food that touches your knee.

My box is fashioned from silver and ice,
The silver seashells look quite nice,
The thread is weaved from human hand,
With the finest thread in all the land.

I will swim in my box,
In the deep crystal sea,
The float aboard a pirate ship,
Where the captain goes by Smee.

Now I will close the magic box.

Rachel Mageean (11)
St Patrick's School, Rochdale

The Magic Box

(Based on 'Magic Box' by Kit Wright)

I will put in the box . . .
The feel of a rabbit, small and cuddly,
The colour from a bright red pen,
The smell of freshly-cut grass.

I will put in the box . . .
The feel of the ice-cold wind against your skin,
A sip of the sweetest fruits,
A round bright moon in the deep blue sky.

I will put in the box . . .
Three precious wishes spoken in Turkish,
The last word spoken by my mum and dad
The first laugh of a baby girl.

I will put in the box . . .
The thirteenth month of the year and the purpleness of the clouds,
A princess in a dungeon
And a slave in a castle.

My box is fashioned from gold, silver
And a lock of hair from a princess,
With hearts on the lid and cobwebs in the corners,
The lock is made from a fossil of a sea turtle.

I shall make my box into a rocket,
Travel through space as fast as lightning,
Then land on a distant planet,
Where there is only good that happens to all!

Laura Davies
St Patrick's School, Rochdale

The Magic Box

(Based on 'Magic Box' by Kit Wright)

I will put in my box . . .
The roar of a lion, soft and warm,
The bark of a dog, loud and soft,
A rainbow of bright colours.

I will put in my box . . .
The sound of a cat purring,
A sip of the lemon of the forest fruits,
A sparkling star in the darkness.

I will put in my box . . .
The first kick of a baby boy,
The last tear from a baby girl,
The first step of a baby.

I will put in my box . . .
A fish in a tree
And a cat in the sea,
The brown of the sky
And the blue of the house.

My box is fashioned from
The feathers of a peacock
And covered with gold from a pirate's chest,
It stands on delicate seashells.

I shall surf in my box
The whole Atlantic Ocean,
Then wash ashore on an orange beach,
The colour of the sun.

Coral O'Keefe (11)
St Patrick's School, Rochdale

Secret Window

Mort was nervous
But yet was hiding
Writing reams that turn out to be the same
Personality finding
The ending is important
Resolution is known
Turning out to be madness
When there is no stories the same
No finding of personality
Yet no hiding, no nerve
Just nothing
Only the ending
And I'm sure in time
Her death will be a mystery
Even to
Me.

Rhiannon Clarke (11)
St Paul's CE Primary School, Adlington

My School

My school
Is cool
I wish they had a swimming pool

The head teacher is Mrs France
She likes to have a dance
I think I'll take a chance

My teacher is Mrs Wingeatt
She's a really good mate
She's never ever late

I have a best friend called Ellie
She is not smelly
She has a sister called Kelly.

Laura Rogers (10)
St Paul's CE Primary School, Adlington

There's Something Up The Stairs

There's something upstairs
What is it? What is it?
It will fulfil your nightmares
Don't scream, don't scream.

It's in your room
What is it? What is it?
It's your doom
Don't scream, don't scream.

Don't look down
What is it? What is it?
You can't help but frown
Don't scream, don't scream.

Phew, it's just a ghost,
Wait! A ghost!
Argh!

Charlotte Stobbs (11)
St Paul's CE Primary School, Adlington

Oliver

In the stables near my house,
A giant shire horse stands.
We feed him fruit and vegetables
From our very soft hands.

I used to think he would bite me,
Now I know he won't.
I always go to the stables
And stroke his lovely coat.

I feel like I can talk to him,
Whenever I get lonely,
He is very cute,
He's my very favourite pony.

Rachel Hindley (11)
St Paul's CE Primary School, Adlington

My Mum Won't Let Me Have A Pet

My mum won't let me keep a parrot
She won't let me keep a rat
She won't let me keep a rhino
Or even an elephant

I'm not allowed to keep horses
And I can't keep snakes
I can't keep koalas
Or tigers with cakes

She won't let me keep a hippo
Or snake's venom in the house
She won't let me keep a duckling
Or a woodlouse

She won't let me keep a lizard
Even in a great big tub
Why can't I keep zebras,
Starfish or a cub?

My mum won't let me have a pet
She knows I'm really keen
I've tried to beg her into it
But she always says, 'In your teens.'

Lucy Fishwick (10)
St Paul's CE Primary School, Adlington

Space

Space, space, space
Is such an amazing place,
Satellites, planets and stars
From Pluto to Mars,
Sun and moon are big and bright,
They block out the darkness of night,
Pluto is small,
Jupiter is tall,
Mission rockets go,
People don't believe in the UFO.

Helen Slater & Abigail O'Brien (9)
St Thomas CE Primary School, Leigh

Holidays

Holidays are fun,
Lazing in the sun,
Lots of ice cream,
Oh what a dream.

Building sandcastles on the beach,
Bodies turning red,
Instead of pale peach.

Out for tea,
Near the sea,
The sun is going down,
But I will never frown.

Here's to the next day,
Out in the bay
And I am going to play.

The holidays have to end,
Send a letter to my friend.
I am coming home,
I am not going to moan.

Jessica Unsworth (7)
St Thomas CE Primary School, Leigh

Space

Aliens are green and spotty,
Sometimes wise, sometimes dumb
And other times they have a third thumb,
Aliens are mean but they're never clean.

The sun's big,
Pluto's small,
There's a great big difference in them all,
Saturn's orange,
The moon's grey,
Get me in a rocket and
Up and away!

Ryan Hodgkinson (9)
St Thomas CE Primary School, Leigh

Fairies

Fairies dance,
Fairies sparkle,
Fairies wish,
Fairies wave their wands
And give wishes.

Fairies dance around
The moon like
Twinkling stars
In the night
And the moon loves it

Fairies fly around
You making sparkles
With your wands
And we love it
We love kind fairies

Fairies dance around
The moon like
Twinkling stars
In the night
And the moon loves it

Fairies, I love fairies
Fairies give me lots of
Great wishes
They tell me fairy stories
About adventure in fairyland

Fairies dance around
The moon like
Twinkling stars in the night
And the moon loves it.

Ruby Taylor (7)
St Thomas CE Primary School, Leigh

Dolphins

Dolphins, dolphins in the sea
Dolphins, dolphins jump at me
Dolphins, dolphins play with me
Dolphins always sing to me

Dolphins, dolphins in the sea
Dolphins, dolphins look at me
I stroke them and they smile back
When I found them I was on her back

Dolphins, dolphins come closer to me
Dolphins, dolphins move away from me
Dolphins, dolphins stare at me
Dolphins always smile at me

Dolphins, dolphins in the sea
Dolphins, dolphins look at me
I stroke them and they smile back
When I found them I was on her back

Dolphins, dolphins swimming free
Dolphins, dolphins swim with me
Dolphins, dolphins swim together
Dolphins, dolphins swim forever

Dolphins, dolphins in the sea
Dolphins, dolphins look at me
I stroke them and they smile back
When I found them I was on her back.

Joanna Morris (7)
St Thomas CE Primary School, Leigh

My Celebrity World

My celebrity world is a very fabulous world,
There is a funky pink hill
And on the pink hill there is a purple hotel,
In the purple hotel lives Britney Spears,
Across the road from the pink hill
There is a blue street with only five houses,
In these houses live . . .
Mis-Teeq, Harry Potter, Ron, Hermione and Girls Aloud,
There is a beauty salon which is multicoloured
And the Spice Girls are dressing in their fashion.

On the main road, the wall next to the salon
Is being painted by Pink, in red, blue, lilac and gold,
There are yellow mountains where lots of old celebrities climb,
That is my celebrity world!

Heather Garfin (9)
St Thomas CE Primary School, Leigh

Pets

Hamsters bite, hamsters nibble
And hamsters wriggle!
Rabbits hop, rabbits run,
Rabbits avoid the farmer's gun!

Gerbils hide, gerbils eat,
Gerbils have stinky, smelly feet!

Dogs bark, dogs wail,
Dogs wag their golden tail!

Cats scratch, cats purr,
Cats have long ginger hair!

Fish swim, fish blow,
Fish just row and row!

Luke Godfrey & Rayyah (9)
St Thomas CE Primary School, Leigh

The Stars And The Moon

The moon was shining like the moonlight,
The people down on Earth looked up at the night.
The moonlight made the night bright
And so made the stars bright too.

The stars,
The stars,
The stars.

How the night is bright,
The night is up in the air,
The stars shine like a very shiny diamond.

A diamond,
A diamond,
A diamond.

The moon did not want them to play,
The moon said, 'Go away!'
The stars went to play
On the planets.

The planets,
The planets,
The planets.

Emma Taberner (7)
St Thomas CE Primary School, Leigh

Mum's Day In Bed

Mum never gets a day off work,
She's always busy,
So today is her first,
This is why she is now still in bed.

Her face is so red and blotchy,
She's got a high temperature,
That's why she's really in bed,
She's not really resting, she's ill instead.

Adam Wilkes (9)
St Thomas CE Primary School, Leigh

Mum's Day In Bed

Our mum has stayed in bed,
She sent her pet animals out instead,
There's . . .
A hedgehog to pick up all the fallen rubbish,
A toad to do the dirty washing up,
A hamster to nibble and sharpen the pencils,
An electric eel to supply and make the electrical power,
A cockerel to act as an alarm clock to wake me up,
A dragon to make the fire but not burn the house down,
A spider to weave the knit and darn the socks,
An elephant to water the flowers,
A cow to make the cheese and milk,
A peacock bird to dust the cabinets with its feathers,
A dog to guard the garden, barking and growling,
An owl to tidy the bookshelf,
An octopus to cook several meals at a time,
A slithering snake to polish the marble floor,
A crocodile to eat the salesmen who call uninvited
And an alligator to help him to open the door,
A rabbit to straighten the cushions which are on the floor,
I bet you never knew just how much Mum had to do.

Amy Boardman & Alexandra Drake (9)
St Thomas CE Primary School, Leigh

The Star And The Sun

One day the sun and the star
Were playing by the moon, moon, moon,
Every day they got up
And played by the moon, moon, moon.

They made a lot of noise by the moon, moon, moon,
One day he got cross
And shouted, 'Go away!'
But day after day
The sun and the star
Continued to play.

Amy Waugh (8)
St Thomas CE Primary School, Leigh

Brothers

I never could understand my brother,
He always got told off by my mother,
My brother is a pest,
He always thinks he's the best,
He doesn't share
And he doesn't care,
He always drives me around the twist
And once he even broke my wrist,
He always beats me up
And broke my favourite cup,
He always tells lies,
My brother really likes pork pies,
My brother cheats at every game,
He was bad when my neighbour came,
My brother takes my toys
And makes too much noise,
He has a spud gun
And always tries to shoot the sun,
He scribbles all over the walls
And nicks everyone's bouncy balls
He always pulls my hair
And he always likes to swear
He always tries to kill the cat
And he never wipes his feet on the mat
But really he's the best brother I have ever had.

Laura Mulcahy & Georgia Smallshaw (9)
St Thomas CE Primary School, Leigh

School

School is horrible
Our school is a terrible disgrace
It is a prison for the day
Where they lock children away
So you see, help us please
And take school away for the day
It would be more fun
If you would change the teachers
To clowns so we would not
Have frowns.

School is a place to get parents
As far away as possible from me
But instead of a clown, maybe me?
Or maybe a flea circus but we would not see
But at least the kids would be the teachers
And I would be the Head
And we would be in control of the teachers instead
But tomorrow it will be back to normal
So there is no use dreaming
So when I am older I will be a teacher
And I can stop dreaming.

Jack Morris & Catherine Buckley (9)
St Thomas CE Primary School, Leigh

Dogs

Dogs are cute,
Dogs play the flute,
Dogs play with you,
So why don't you
Think of a dog?
Is it a man's best friend?
Well, mine isn't, it barks,
Bites and it even opens the fridge, sneaky dog!

There are fat dogs,
Ugly dogs just like old dogs,
There are nice dogs, bad dogs, just like the guard dogs,
There are playful dogs and miserable dogs just like me.

Sam Pollard (9)
St Thomas CE Primary School, Leigh

Black

Black is a cat in the misty dark,
Black is a creepy distant bark.

Black is a witch's cape and hat,
Black is a sleeping upside down bat.

Black is a sad, mean thing,
Black won't make you feel like you want to sing.

Black is an old sewing machine,
That will never be used or seen.

Alexandra Finch (7)
St Wilfrid's CE Primary School, Ribchester

Animals Are Everywhere!

Animals are everywhere
What shall I do?
Should I pour water over the cat
Or should I dress it in a hat?
Animals are everywhere
What shall I do?
Shall I give the dog fake food
Or shall I put it in a mood?
Animals are everywhere
What shall I do?
Should I scare the rabbit away
Or should I give it a poisonous carrot?

Isabella Fabbrini (7)
St Wilfrid's CE Primary School, Ribchester

What's The Weather?

Yesterday it was rainy,
Last week it was windy,
Today it is hailing,
Tomorrow it will be galey,
Oh when can it be sunny?
Next week it will be stormy,
The week after that will be a hurricane,
Oh when can it be sunny?
In the holidays it's cold,
The week after that it will be snowing.
Hurrah, it's sunny!

Anna Gavan (7)
St Wilfrid's CE Primary School, Ribchester

Snow, Sweet Snow

I love snow
Cold drops of water
Frozen water

Shiver, shiver, shiver!

My cat's paw prints
In the snow
Off you go

Oh no!
Summer's coming
Goodbye snow.

Heather Pye (7)
St Wilfrid's CE Primary School, Ribchester

Clockwork

Clockwork, clockwork
How does it work?
Is there a hamster turning the hands around?
Clockwork, clockwork,
How does it work?
Is there a battery that knows the time?

Matthew Swinburne (7)
St Wilfrid's CE Primary School, Ribchester

Spirits

Spirits are like fluttering dreams,
Spirits are like the water in streams,
Spirits are like the air in a breath,
Spirits are there when it's time for death.

Grace Feehan (9)
Sacred Heart RC Primary School

Children Of The Week

Monday's child is always naughty
Tuesday's child is writing poetry
Wednesday's child is really funny
Thursday's child lost his bunny
Friday's child has a big cake
Saturday's child has a pet snake
But the child that was born on the seventh day
Is good and kind so that is OK.

Ciaran Gannon (9)
Sacred Heart RC Primary School

Haikus

Seashells on the shore
The sea quietly clashing
And crashing the sand

Stop, the lights turned red
Up the street and passed the shops
At school, so get out.

Elizabeth Robinson (9)
Sacred Heart RC Primary School

Sporty Poem

Athletics, you must run real fast
Basketball, the ball dribbles right past
Cricket, the men all wear white
Discus, the disc is in flight
Extreme, be careful you don't fall
Football, score a great goal.

Ella Ogden (8)
Sacred Heart RC Primary School

Nature Poems

Lost cloud
Resting against the wind
Morning is over

Bright moon
Floating over the water
The night is coming

Delicate flower
Stands upon the hill
Summer is beginning.

Chloe Roscoe (9)
Sacred Heart RC Primary School

Ruins Of Wycoller

We are the stone finders
We are the ruins of a castle
We are the fireplace lights
We are the steps of a castle
We are the wide pillars
We are the window of lines
We are the stone carvers.

Zacharia Jordan Kaye (8)
Sacred Heart RC Primary School

Badger

I am the coal stealer
I am the shield scratcher
Ruins scratcher
Grass rooter.

Harry Kaye (8)
Sacred Heart RC Primary School

Love Is Special

Roses are red, just as your cheeks
I think you are special to me
Because of the way you look at me
I can't explain my love for you
I go crazy when I look at you

I can't think of anything to say
I blush when I see you
I go so red that my face is redder than my heart.

Mellisa Hind (9)
Sacred Heart RC Primary School

Little Grey Squirrel

I run across the ground;
I don't make a sound.
I quickly scamper up the tree
And gather acorns . . . one, two, three

I sit on branches and look around
I gather acorns that I've found
I'm a grey, old fella with a bushy tail
I tried to catch but to no avail.

Molly Frankland (9)
Sacred Heart RC Primary School

Pendle Witch

Scary! Hairy!
Not necessary,
Or ordinary.
Hook nose,
Fire eyes.

Connor Hennessy-King (9)
Sacred Heart RC Primary School

Night Breeze

Little flower
Growing upon the hill
Springtime!

Bright moon
Always shining
Upon the sky!

Strange leaves
Dancing with the wind
Night breeze!

Lost cloud
Standing behind the mist
Cold time!

Fintan Rowan Young (8)
Sacred Heart RC Primary School

Alphabet Names

(An extract)

A is for Amanda who is the naughty girl
B is for Brooklyn who has a big curl
C is for Claire who is very rude
D is for Dory who runs around nude
E is for Ella who is very kind
F is for Florry who doesn't mind.

Yasmin Bracewell (9)
Sacred Heart RC Primary School

Wycoller Bridge

I am big . . . made of stone,
I stay in the same place all the time!
People walk across me,
Water under me.

Jessica Ayers (9)
Sacred Heart RC Primary School

Wintry Day At School

One day I was walking to school
On a wintry day and everything was cool
Teachers getting stressy

Wintry, wintry
Silly, silly
Cold, cold
Wintry day at school

Wintry day at school, all cold, all snow
Everyone making the snowballs
Teachers are mad, snow scattered all over everything
Stinks of snow, everything is like a spacesuit

Wintry, wintry
Silly, silly
Cold, cold
Wintry day at school

Glistening snowflakes all around, glowing outside
In the wintry day everyone happy, every day
Blizzard starting, everyone going home
Chucking snowballs, everyone messing around
Everyone naughty, everyone getting done by their mum

Wintry, wintry
Silly, silly
Cold, cold
Wintry day at school.

Shaun McArdle-Watson (8)
Sacred Heart RC Primary School

Tree

Leaf-thrower,
Branch-grower,
Worm-lover,
Leaf-grower,
People-hater!

Harry Kavanagh (8)
Sacred Heart RC Primary School

Gardener's Friend

I am a leaf-eater,
A little flyer,
I am a spotty creature,
A female bird, a quick flyer,
I show beautiful patterns on my wings,
I belong to the summer spirit!

Rachel Curran (9)
Sacred Heart RC Primary School

Barn Owl

Silent flyer
Turning head
My call of death
Mice catcher!

Alex Bailey (9)
Sacred Heart RC Primary School

The Cheetah

Charging through the jungle,
As fast as fast can be,
The cheetah looks around him,
But there isn't much to see.

Just a blurry world,
All colours smudged together,
The world is just a coloured blizzard,
In the worst of weather.

Georgina Abram (11)
Sherwood Primary School

If I Had A Million Pounds . . .

If I had a million pounds,
Golden coins in massive mounds,
Or a suitcase with notes in right to the top,
Right to the top, like it'd never ever stop . . .

If I had that amount of dosh,
I'd be just like the Queen, but even more posh!
I'd be content lazing around on cloud nine,
No problems, no hardships, everything fine . . .

If I had that much money,
I'd be playing in my cool pool, when it was sunny,
If it wasn't warm, I'd splash indoors,
I'd have a fun school where the staff weren't bores!

Actually, to be honest 'bout this,
My slave would be my big sis
And I'd spend all my cash on
Sugary, scrumptious, sensational . . .
Sweets!

Sameera Auckburally (10)
Sherwood Primary School

My Little Sister

Her cheeks are bright and as red as a rose,
She bites her nails and sucks her toes,
She continuously reaches for the cookie jar,
Until she realises she won't get far.

She walks about in her little black shoes,
She pesters Dad when he's watching the news,
She stomps through puddles and plays with our cat,
Then leaves lots of mud on the front doormat.

Emily Bradley (11)
Sherwood Primary School

The Four Seasons

Spring is here,
So let's give a cheer,
Baby chicks are born,
The sun rises at the time of dawn.

Summer is here,
So let's give a cheer,
This is the best time of the year!
Children play happily in the sun,
Whilst everyone else enjoys the fun.

Autumn is here,
So let's give a cheer,
Leaves fall to the ground,
Lots of colours all around.

Winter is here,
So let's give a cheer,
Hail and snowstorms all around,
Soon the green leaves will be found.

Charlotte Bamber (11)
Sherwood Primary School

Night

Night comes swiftly, floating here and there
He sweeps his cloak round the hallway,
Heading for my room
He knocks quietly on my bedroom wall
With that, in the darkness, he binds
The door and squeezes through the keyhole

He creeps stealthily up to the window
Making images with blinds
Night creeps along the wall devouring the light
Then he leaps on the floor and extinguishing the light
Pounces here and there making
Things vanish into thin air.

Laurie Cameron (9)
Sherwood Primary School

The Cookie Jar Dilemma

Like a fish drawn to water,
I edge nearer and nearer to the cookie jar,
Mouth watering, knees clenching.

Mum leaves the kitchen, alone and vulnerable
And the cookie jar stands tall on the shelf,
Mouth watering, knees clenching.

I peer down the hall, all is safe,
Reaching for the stepladder, my heart skips,
Mouth watering, knees clenching.

Closer . . . closer . . . I reach out,
Footsteps in the hall, oh no,
Mouth dry, knees knocking.

The queen of all, screams and shouts,
She bawls and baffles,
Mouth watering, knees knobbly.

Mary Clayton (11)
Sherwood Primary School

What Is God?

Someone to rely on whenever down,
He will always forgive you,
Even if you do wrong,
You'll never know if he's around,
But he watches every step you make.

How could you hide from the man up there?
He's in the forest, on top of the mountains,
Under the ocean and in the sky,
He's even in your little house.

Francesca Deaville (11)
Sherwood Primary School

Alone

The ice-cold water doesn't bother me,
But having no friends is the problem,
The sharks play catch with all the little fish,
All I do is wonder alone,
I cannot hide and have nowhere to go,
My diary is free every night,
Yes, that is right, I am a big old whale . . .
With no friends.

Emma Cook (10)
Sherwood Primary School

Families

F ather is a walking workshop who fixes things for you.
A unties and uncles care about you too.
M um is a big teddy bear that you cuddle up to when you are sad.
I f you are ill your family helps you get better.
L ove your grandparents, even though they may not be there.
I deas in my head are planted by my family.
E ven though you may fight, brothers and sisters are important.
S mile, cheer up, your family is the most important thing in your life.

Emily Kay (11)
Sherwood Primary School

What Is The Moon?

It is a white boat floating in the night sky,
It is a white banana hanging off the night sky,
It is a white bowl of hope,
It is a pale face of peace,
What is the moon?
It is a white boat floating in the night sky.

Daniel Duckworth (11)
Sherwood Primary School

The World Of Creatures!

High up in the tree,
Sleeps a dreaming koala,
Like a new baby.

Swinging from a branch,
A lively monkey jumps around,
Like a rustling tree.

Over the desert,
Slithers a slippery snake,
Like an oil leak.

Rebecca Fisher (10)
Sherwood Primary School

Sun, Moon And Stars

In the turquoise sky,
Hovers the radiant sun,
Like a hot light bulb.

In the blackened sky,
Floats the quicksilver moon,
Like a new, polished spoon.

In the gloomy sky,
Flickers a cluster of stars,
Like a glittered cloak.

Peter Gawne (11)
Sherwood Primary School

Parrots Haiku

At the canopy,
Parrots flee, sparkling their path
Like fashion in town.

Mohammed Mitha (11)
Sherwood Primary School

Safari Creatures

A slender creature
In the plains of the desert
Stands the proud giraffe

A fearsome creature
Beneath the undergrowth
Sits the mighty lion

A wrinkly creature
Bathing in the cool water
The elephant drinks.

Kate Jefferies (11)
Sherwood Primary School

Haikus

High upon the roof
Sadly the cat crouches down
Like a quiet moon

In the old cottage
Grandma stays on the sofa
Like a lazy sloth.

Rabia Khan (11)
Sherwood Primary School

My Grandad

My grandad is the best,
He takes me everywhere.
He takes me to the west,
Then takes me to a fair.
Whenever he's alone,
I comfort him at home.
My grandad will always be the best.

Oliver Nelson (10)
Sherwood Primary School

Spring

The flowers blossom in the sun,
As the children wait for the ice cream man to come.

The crystal stream runs through the valley
And the children find some shade in the alley.

Daffodils dance in the mid-spring's lawn
And the daisies are newly born.

The sparrow lays its new five eggs
And waits to see them pop out their legs.

The spring has come and soon has to go
And the wonderful sights will no longer show.

Tara-Jo Leyland (11)
Sherwood Primary School

What Is Love?

Love is a ball of hearts
Softly entwined together,
Never to depart,
Love is stronger than friendship,
Love is used throughout life,
Everybody has love deep down in their hearts.

Love is when people come together,
Love is a beautiful thing to have,
Love is used for family,
Love can become tears,
Love can become happiness,
Love should be there forever.

Dalton Riley (10)
Sherwood Primary School

Seasons

Trees are growing leaves,
Grass is spreading lush and green,
Animals appear.

Sun is shining bright,
Beaches are full of people,
Parasols are up.

Leaves are falling fast,
Squirrels collect fresh acorns,
Colours are around.

Trees are brown and bare,
The animals hibernate,
White snow starts falling.

Jenny Mortlock (11)
Sherwood Primary School

What Are The Stars?

The stars are gleaming glitter
Laid out onto black paper

Polished money squashed into
A black leather purse

What are the stars?

Silver sequins sparkling
In a black cupboard

When diamonds gleam
And shimmer in a dark shop.

Jade Pike (11)
Sherwood Primary School

Night

Night is a trickster, he betrays you and your eyes,
Then he hides in a corner and waits for your cries.

Night is a creeper, he's unseen but coming,
He creeps up to your bed and sends you running.

Night is a burglar he steals all the light,
He'll make your chair into a monster and deliver you a fright.

Night is a hider concealed behind the desk,
Until tomorrow evening when he wakes for your rest.

Joseph Nithsdale (11)
Sherwood Primary School

My Eleventh Birthday!

Hip hip hooray, it's my birthday today!
I am eleven today,
Hip hip hooray, it's my birthday today!
At four o'clock my party will strike,
Hip hip hooray, it's my birthday today!
The party will be full of fun, dancing and laughter,
Hip hip hooray, it's my birthday today!
The party will finish, I will be another year older,
Hip hip hooray, it's my birthday today!

Melissa Pang (11)
Sherwood Primary School

What Are The Stars?

When glitter is laid on black paper,
When sparkles shine from the moon,
When silver sequins glow in a dark room,
When diamonds shimmer in a dark pitch-black shop,
When money is placed in a black, beautiful purse.

Bethany Leeming (10)
Sherwood Primary School

My Ultimate Pet!

I want a pet that's
As brave as a lion,
As cool as a cat,
As swift as an eagle,
As pretty as a peacock,
As sly as a fox!

My pet would be
Half lion, half cat,
Half an eagle, half peacock,
Just add a bit of fox,
I've got my ultimate pet!

I don't want a pet that's
As dopey as a donkey,
As blind as a bat,
As slow as a sloth,
As mad as a hatter or
As stubborn as a mule!

Rachel Wood (11)
Sherwood Primary School

Autumn

A cold storm,
makes the leaves mourn
and hats and gloves appear.

The crunch comes
and you get cold thumbs,
that's all you need to hear.

Digging in leaves,
they get stuck up your sleeves,
can't stay out long.

Winter's near,
don't fear,
I will stay close.

Rachel Tate (10)
Sherwood Primary School

Great Animals

Up in the tall tree
A great grey koala lay
Like a lost raindrop

Listening so hard
Waits a patient crocodile
Like a drifting log

Up in the blue sky
A bird gently flies along
Like breeze with feathers.

Mark Tate (10)
Sherwood Primary School

Animals Haikus

Along the river,
Swishes by a mighty croc,
Like a crinkled boat.

Flying through the skies,
Flaps a tiny sparrow bird,
Like a small bullet.

Swimming round a bowl,
Splashing around, shiny fish,
Like a block of gold.

Holly Pears (11)
Sherwood Primary School

The Pig Haiku

Through the sty it goes,
A muscley pig running,
Like a moving train.

Duncan Young (10)
Sherwood Primary School

Summer

The golden flames slowly bob up,
As the children come out to play,
Leaves turning all green.

The sun is shining,
Above the people on the beach,
Who are having hot days in the sun.

Waves bobbing up and down, crashing against the rocks,
The children are eating ice lollies,
In the scorching sun.

Jennifer Reilly (10)
Sherwood Primary School

I Could Be . . .

I could be a vet,
Looking after your pet.

I could own a shop
And my shop will be top.

I could be a pop star
And drive a very posh car.

I could drive a car,
All the way to Zanzibar.

Or I could be me,
That's what I'll be!

Emily Trickett (9)
Whalley CE Primary School

The Romans

Romans are tough
Romans are giant
Romans have shields and swords
Big shields
Sharp swords
Shining armour
Romans have posh clothes
Orange ring
Magic druids
Armies are big
Lots of shields
Lots of swords
Run for life
Romans
Are here
Bang
Ow!
Run
For
Your
Life!

Sam Wells (8)
Whalley CE Primary School

My Cat!

My cat is black and white,
He goes out every night,
His eyes glow in the moonlight,
He does a slinky walk
And when he eats he nearly chokes,
As a cat, would he miaows for his talk,
I love my cat because he is all mine.

Megan Jackson (9)
Whalley CE Primary School

Making Medicine For Grandma

I ought to say
That it was May
When I said, 'I will make a medicine'
So give me a bird and a jumping flea
Two snails and lizards three
Four toes in it goes
But hold your nose!
Put in the oil
And a large bit of soil
In goes the smelly cheese
To make her sneeze!
And one hundred other things as well
Each with a rather nasty smell
Will she go pop?
Will she explode?
Will she go soaring
Through the road?
Well, on that day in sunny May
I made a medicine for Grandma.

Kelly Mashiter (8)
Whalley CE Primary School

Colours

Blue is for the misty sky
White is for the clouds up so high
Yellow is for the bright sunshine
Pink is for all the things of mine
Black is for the dark caves
Green is for the sloppy waves
Silver is for the shiny stars
Gold is the things around Mars
Purple is for friendship of best friends
Red is for friendship that never ends
Turquoise is for the fun
Beige is for under the sun.

Sylvie Bowman (8)
Whalley CE Primary School

I Want To Be . . .

I want to be a fairy
and have a glittery wand

I want to be a hairdresser
and cut people's hair

I want to be a mouse
and eat cheese all day

I want to be a knight
in shining armour

I want to be a dinosaur
and roam the land

I want to be a star
and shine from up high

I want to be a princess
and live in a palace

I want to be a teddy
all loved and wanted

I want to be a pirate
and sail the seven seas

I want to be a butterfly
with colourful wings

I want to be a pop star
and sing on stage

I want to be a cloud
and drift away

I want to be a giraffe
and have the tallest neck ever

I want to be just *me!*
That's all I want to be.

Olivia Jackson (11)
Whalley CE Primary School

The Magic Waterfall!

Bubbling cool water flowing over rocks,
Beautiful mermaids with golden locks,
Underneath the cover of foam,
Little creatures love to roam,
From the ceiling of stones fall little drips
And tiny fish do mega flips,
It sparkles and dances in the night
And shimmers and glimmers in the moonlight,
Its bubbles of crystal, its colours of green,
Though the mystery is it's never been seen,
Not even the humans, in planes in the sky
Have ever witnessed it with their eyes,
Magical colours swirl around it
And still no one has ever found it
And now it still does remain a mystery,
The tale will go down, down in history,
A circle of rocks displayed round the bottom,
And no animal has ever forgotten,
The mystical light, the gentle sound,
Splashed water all over the ground,
It greets the animals and the birds,
From pairs of creatures to giant herds,
So never forget the waterfall,
With plenty of clear water installed,
Though the thing you must never tell
Is where the waterfall does dwell
And that's the waterfall's song it sends
And how we've come to a mystical end.

Jessica Wild (9)
Whalley CE Primary School

If You Look Around You

If you look around you, you see the sky and sea,
If you look around you, you have to see you and me.
If you look around you, you see the sun and stars,
If you look around you, you have to see Venus and Mars.

All around is the sea and the sky,
All around us are the bees and the flies,
All around us are you and me,
All around us is our family.

William Lancaster (8)
Whalley CE Primary School

Is It Right?

Is it right that men should kill animals
for their coats, tusks and teeth?

Is it right that men should chop down
trees and not replace them?

Is it right that people should
burgle and murder, harming and hurting?

Is it right that some children in our world
should work for money instead of having an education?

No! No! No!

Ben Wallbank (8)
Wray-With-Botton Endowed School

Lonely Boy

Sitting in the back alley, all wet and shivering,
I, who should be a little boy, snoring in a warm, thick blanket,
Once, I was a little boy cared for and loved,
But now, I am lost
And from now on, I am a lonely child.

John Staveley (8)
Wray-With-Botton Endowed School

Right And Responsibilities

We all have the . . .
Right to education and the teachers that teach us
so that we may work well for our world.
Right to live safely because we want our children to grow up better.
Right to have property and keep the nation tidy,
so that the world does not smell.
Right to have intelligence and learn from it
because then we have brighter brains.
Right to be loyal and have love around,
so that we will be true to others.
Right to have energy and keep fit in our lives,
so that we are not lazy.
Right to play with toys children want to play with
because then children are not going to be sad all the time.
Right to say and speak what people believe in
because they want to practise the religion they want.
Right to do what people want to do and feel free,
so that they have good lives.
Right to entertain and enjoy it
because people need it for a change.
Right to stop war and crime with affects us
because we won't live the lives we want to live.
Right to live where you were brought up
because you will belong to your own country.

Joe Atkinson (9)
Wray-With-Botton Endowed School

Poor

Why are some homey, while others are lonely?
While one man has riches, another lives in ditches,
While some look for food, others have already chewed,
While one country is in peace, another is in pieces,
Why is one man fit and well, when another is sick and ill?
Why does one man get more and more, when another is
                                          very, very poor?

Robert Staveley (11)
Wray-With-Botton Endowed School

Peace

Peace is the blue sky,
Peace is the bright, hot, summer sun,
Peace is the green grass.

War is the hard gun,
War is the army men shooting,
War is the dark sky.

Peace is the woolly sheep,
Peace is the skipping of lambs,
Peace is the cows calling.

War is the children crying,
War is the robbing from banks,
War is the bullets, hurting.

Esther Preece (10)
Wray-With-Botton Endowed School

My Angel Of Peace

Peace is my angel;
peace flies in the bright blue sky,
peace is my Heaven.

It is hard, very,
for my angel to spread peace;
we need to help her.

We can stop violence;
we must share and care;
help my peace angel.

Tamsin Seed (9)
Wray-With-Botton Endowed School

Seasons

Spring

Winter over,
Flowers waking,
Trees budding,
Little showers,
New life.

Summer

Summer holiday now,
Sitting in the sun,
Suncream on,
Nice and bright,
Going to a foreign country.

Autumn

Going back to school,
Trees losing leaves,
We jump in piles,
Conkers to collect,
Getting near to winter.

Winter

Snowflakes falling from the sky,
Presents to open soon,
Snowball fights,
Snowmen towns,
We have nips in our fingers and toes.

Lois Preece (8)
Wray-With-Botton Endowed School

Rights And Wrongs

Is it right to judge people before we get to know them
or because they are different?
Is it wrong to express our feelings and opinion
or speak our mind within reason?
Is it right to kill others for our own mistakes
or make others suffer for our own stupidity?
Is it wrong to act with frustration and anger
or to dwell on the past that lies behind us
instead of looking to the future that lies before us?

If there is one man against others,
that man will not survive.
If there is a dozen men with that one man,
together they are strong; remember, wrongs cannot make it right!

Lily Hughes (11)
Wray-With-Botton Endowed School

Homeless

H elpful: be helpful to your friends and you will have a better life.
O thers: others are more important, think of others before yourself.
M eanness: don't treat people like they aren't human, everyone
   should be treated the same way.
E ducation: everyone needs an education to have a full life,
   you can't get a good job if you don't have an education.
L iving: everyone needs a home because the streets aren't good
   enough for humans.
E ntertainment: if everyone has a fun life you will have a good life too.
S afety: parents should look after children because
   children are special.
S mile: always smile and you will make everyone happier.

Virginia Hartley (10)
Wray-With-Botton Endowed School